THE LASCAUX NOTEBOOKS

The Lascaux Notebooks

JEAN-LUC CHAMPERRET

EDITED & TRANSLATED BY
PHILIP TERRY

CARCANET CLASSICS

First published in Great Britain in 2022 by
Carcanet
Alliance House, 30 Cross Street
Manchester, M2 7AQ
www.carcanet.co.uk

A CIP catalogue record for this book is
available from the British Library.

ISBN 978 1 80017 172 5

Book design by Andrew Latimer
Printed in Great Britain by SRP Ltd, Exeter, Devon

The publisher acknowledges financial
assistance from Arts Council England.

'Quantity over quality.'
– Jean-Luc Champerret, *Carnet Gris*

CONTENTS

In August 2006 I was on holiday in Charentes with my family, trying to finish off a translation of a novel by Catherine Axelrad on Victor Hugo, *L'Enfant d'Aurigny*. When our holiday let expired, towards the end of August, as we still had a few days free, we decided to prolong our vacation, as was our custom, by spending a couple of nights with an architect friend, David Martin, who lived near Montignac in the village of La Bachellerie. We saw very little of our friend, as it happened – as usual, he was burning the candle at both ends, and he was in the middle of a complicated job converting the interior of a nearby château, which had been acquired by a wealthy Japanese client whose enormous wealth was matched only by his stringency. He talked at length about the project, which had been taking up his time for some months, even showing us his architect's drawing plans. Essentially, he was leaving the exterior intact, as he had to, for it was an *immeuble classé*, but was remodelling the interior *à la japonaise* – which, as far as I can remember, consisted in knocking down a lot of walls, inserting new supports, installing a zen-like courtyard garden with a fountain constructed according to principles derived from the *I Ching*, and erecting a large number of white silk partitions supported by bamboo in place of the walls. He was discussing this with us on the terrace on the last evening over a bottle of Margaux when, just before he went to bed, he suddenly said 'I have somethiing for you'. At which point he rushed down to his cellar and came back, minutes later, not with the bottle of vintage wine we had been anticipating, but with a large and rather dirty wooden crate. 'This,' he said, 'is yours. I found it tucked away at the back of a cupboard in the château. They're the papers of a local poet who used to live there, Jean-Luc Champerret. They might interest you

– and they're of no use to me. Have you heard of him?' I had not – but I willingly disburdened him of the crate, which we squeezed into our already packed car in the morning.

When we got home, I put the box in the garage without opening it, for in truth I was not much interested in French regional poets that neither I nor anyone else had heard of, and thought no more about it. Over the next four years I was preoccupied with administrative duties back home as the university sector, where I earned my living, became increasingly corporate. There were the usual cuts and closures – 'rationalisation' was the word they used – the usual cull of senior staff, the usual restructurings, and then, as a certain satirical poem drawing comparisons between the vice-chancellor and Stalin was leaked on Facebook, I was forced to adopt a low profile for a period, busying myself with visiting lectureships and secondments.[1] It wasn't until June 2009 that I looked at the crate again. After returning from a teaching

---

1 Now that the storm has blown over, it is perhaps the right moment to print the poem in full, not least because various, and much more scatological, versions of the verses were circulated at the time without my knowledge or approval. The verses, it goes without saying, are in imitation of Mandelstam's unpropitious poem on Stalin, which led to his imprisonment and exile. I am indebted to Professor Angela Livingstone for clarifying Mandelstam's Russian. The correct title of the poem is 'Five Year Plan': 'We are alive but no longer feel the campus under our feet,/you can't hear what we say from ten steps away//but when anyone half-starts a conversation/they mention the military man from Durham.//His thick fingers are like worms,/his words bark at you like hounds.//His cockroach brows laugh,/and the top-knot of his tie shines.//He is surrounded by his bald-headed henchmen,/and clowns with his large spotted handkerchief.//Someone nods, someone smiles, another pie chart is projected,/he alone points at us and thunders.//He forges order after order like hand grenades,/hurling them at the cleaners,

stint in Berlin, where I had been helping them set up a Creative Writing programme at the *Freie Universität*, we were preparing to move house – we'd decided to downsize as our son would soon be going off to university – and sorting through some junk in the garage I came across the Champerret box again. This time, I opened it – partly out of curiosity, partly to determine whether or not I should throw it in the skip that was taking up the drive. It wasn't all that easy to open – the lid had been nailed down with some veritable *clous paysans* – but once I got it off I examined the contents. It contained papers, some loose, some tied in bundles, covered all over with thick brown dust, a few rusty ink pens, some pieces of charcoal, several bundles of letters, three small notebooks – one black, one grey, and one blue – and six copies of a volume of poems by Champerret, *Chants de la Dordogne*, published by a small press in Perigueux in 1941, *Éditions du Noir* (presumably a reference to Perigord Noir, the old *pays* name, still in use, for the region which lies to the south of Perigueux, and which takes its name from the black oaks which grow there). The volume contained a collection of rather sonorous poems – reminiscent of Swinburne in this respect – written in rhyming alexandrines, seemingly based on, or attempting to recreate, peasant songs from the region, celebrating robust country life and a now vanished mode of smallholder farming, where a single farm would produce its own *foie gras, confit d'oie, truffes*, goat's cheese, wine, and a regional version of *eau de vie* distilled from acorns called *eau de chêne*. The papers themselves, or some of them at least, were in a fragile state, and some of the loose leaves collapsed when you picked them up, turning to dust – it looked, too, like a family of mice had at one time made their home in the crate, using the paper to make a nest.

-----

the administrators, the professors.//The broad-breasted boss from the north/savours each early retirement like an exquisite sweet.'

The papers that had survived included notes, and more poems, written in much shorter lines, accompanied by diagrams reminiscent of Chinese calligraphy, and a number of abstract drawings in charcoal done on standard issue *Bureau de Poste* blank postcards, a little like some of the graphic work of Henri Michaux. There were also a number of visual poems where the words and letters were distributed sparsely across the page in various font sizes, perhaps indebted to Apollinaire, certainly influenced by Mallarmé's *Un Coup de dés*, of which they seemed to be a somewhat belated imitation. The *Carnet Gris*, the first I opened, bore the title '*Notes sur Lascaux*', and was written in pencil. The first 36 pages were filled with writing and diagrams in a diminutive and impenetrable script. The rest of the notebook was blank. I closed the crate, sure of one thing – it was not going in the skip.[2]

Subsequently, I tried to find out more about Jean-Luc Champerret, but it was not easy. There was little on public record – no trace of his *Chants de la Dordogne* remained, and the Bibliothèque Nationale did not hold a single copy. Nor did he appear to have written any other published works. And when I asked my few contacts in French Departments – David Bellos, John Sturrock, Cécile de Bary – none of them had heard of him. I did, however, track down his birth certificate via the *Mairie* in Montignac. He was born in the village of Le Moustier, on the road from Les Eyzies to Montignac, on 11 September 1910, to Alice Rose Champerret and Gaston Yves Champerret. But there was nothing more. Clutching at straws, I rang David Martin, to see if he had any more information on Champerret, and he was able to put me in touch with

---

2 The contents of the Champerret box are now held in the archives of the Pôle de la Préhistoire in Les Eyzies, where they are stored in three box files, the *Boîte Noire* (B.N.), the *Boîte Rouge* (B.R.), and the *Boîte Jaune* (B.J.).

one Isabelle Dupois, who had worked as a housemaid at the château where the crate had been found. At once I travelled down to the Dordogne to meet her. She was a little lady, now of an advanced age, who was hard of hearing but who had no faith in modern hearing aids, so that you had to raise your voice to get through to her, and could only ask the simplest of questions. However, she was able to furnish me with the following information. Champerret had been living in Paris at the outbreak of the war where, she believed, he had briefly worked in the Resistance, working with a cell that included a tall wiry Irishman, before being forced to flee from the capital, at which point he had returned to his native region. Here, he had taken up residence at the château, which at that point had been requisitioned by the local Resistance. He was a quiet man, who didn't give much away, but she knew from what she had gathered at the time that he had worked, among other things, as a code breaker. When Lascaux was discovered by five schoolboys and their dog Robot, on 12 September 1940, Champerret had been sent in secret by his cell to survey the caves, in case they offered a possible hideout for Resistance members. But nothing came of this plan, as within days everyone in the area knew about the discovery of a new and remarkable set of cave paintings in the hills to the south of Montignac. Then in February 1942 the château was raided by the Gestapo. Champerret got away, but Dupois knew nothing of his subsequent movements. 'Did he ever marry?' I asked her. 'Non,' she replied emphatically, 'ce n'était pas sons genre.'

It was the notebooks, I soon learnt, that supplied the key to Champerret's work. What is certain, is that during his clandestine excursion to Lascaux, made before any archaeologists had set foot there, Champerret had not only evaluated the potential of the network of caves for Resistance operations, but had looked very closely at the paintings, and had looked particularly at the signs and marks, seeing in their ancient forms a hidden code. During his long, lonely, nervous nights at the château, Champerret must have ruminated on what he had seen in the cave, bringing his skills as a code-breaker to bear on the ancient drawings and signs, and the notebooks contained the rich fruit of these ruminations. The notebooks are not always easy to decipher. At the best of times they are difficult to read, then some of the pages are missing, many are blank, and at apparently crucial points the pages seem to have been chewed up by rodents. And then, they are notebooks. The arguments are not made or advanced at all systematically. Nevertheless, putting it all together, Champerret's propositions relating to what he saw in the caves of Lascaux, seem to be along the following lines. Focussing primarily on the signs that he found there – signs that subsequent generations have almost unanimously defined as uninterpretable – Champerret at once proposes that they are to be read as script, as a primitive form of writing, and in the last pages of the *Carnet Bleu* he proposes meanings that should be attached to each sign. A row of vertical lines, he proposes, might represent spears, or a forest, or even rain. An upturned 'v' sign (or, rather, two such signs, one on top of the other) might represent mountains, or huts. A line of dots might represent people, or a journey, or faces, or stars. A row of horizontal lines might represent mist or night. A sign resembling an upturned question mark might represent a club, a sign resembling a three-quarters circle with a dot in the middle, an eye, a meandering line or group of lines a river, and so on. *'Le signe,'* he remarks at one point – suggesting that the ideas of Saussure, which were to influence a subsequent generation writing on Lascaux[3], had already crossed the

---

3 Among the best-known examples of a structuralist approach to cave art is André Leroi-Gourhan's monumental *Treasures of Prehistoric Art*, translated by Norbert Guterman (New York: Abrams, 1967). Here, in

Swiss border by word of mouth – '*n'est jamais arbitraire*'. Such signs, he argues, could be linked together in sequence to form primitive sentences or to carry or pass on messages, were they to be scratched on a stone or a piece of bark, or even scratched in the earth with a stick. Or they might just make a record of a transaction between tribes. So, the sign for mountains in conjunction with the sign for journey would convey, for example, that a hunting party had crossed the mountains. A group of signs representing antlers might record the goods handed over in an exchange.[4]

This, in itself, amounts to a revolutionary breakthrough in interpreting the signs found in the caves at Lascaux, when we think that in 1986, 46 years after Champerret composed his notes, Mario Ruspoli, in his book *The Cave of Lascaux*, could write 'the signs are unfathomably mysterious'.[5] And yet, Champerret's imagination by no means stops here. In what is no doubt his most radical step, he draws our attention to the curious, but frequent, three by three grids of squares that decorate the walls of the cave, most notably in the polychrome

---

what now seems like an example of the reductive tendency in structuralism, which led to the movement towards post-sructuralism, Leroi-Gourhan, in an act of interpretation that Derrida would subsequently come to term *phallocentric*, reads all the cave drawings and all the accompanying signs as examples of either the masculine (the phallus) or the feminine (the vulva).

4 When I gave a paper on Champerret at the University of Essex conference 'Translation: A Walk on the Wild Side' in June 2017, Simon Everett, a CHASE-funded PhD student who was giving a paper on untranslatability in Mandarin poetry, remarked that several of the signs in Champerret, such as that for mountain, closely resembled the symbols in oracle bone script (the origin of Chinese pictographic script).

5 Mario Ruspoli *The Cave of Lascaux: The Final Photographs* transl. Sebastian Wormell (London: Thames and Hudson, 1987), p. 160.

blazon below the Black Cow in the Nave of Lascaux. Taking a leap of the imagination, a leap in the dark – and is this not quite literally what the bounding Chinese horses lining the ceiling of Lascaux's Axial Gallery ask us to do by example? – Champerret proposes that these grids, in themselves empty of meaning, act as frameworks for the insertion of signs, thereby acquiring and multiplying meanings. Just as the signs for mountain and journey, placed in conjunction, acquire meanings, so the grid filled with signs, and scratched, for example, on a stone, might carry messages. So, the grid filled with antlers might represent a large consignment of antlers, the grid filled with signs representing the forest and signs for fire might warn of a forest fire. But Champerret goes further than this, proposing that whereas these grids might have originally been used for practical purposes, that they evolved to form the basis of the first written poetry. Of course, this is an astonishing, almost unbelievable proposition, in effect announcing the discovery of Ice Age poetry. But if *Homo sapiens fossilis* could create visual art, both parietal and mobiliary, that would inspire some of the greatest painters and sculptors of the twentieth century – from Picasso and Dubuffet to Pierre Soulanges, Marcel Duchamp and Louise Bourgeois – and if such people could, as has recently been argued, create the origins of cinema in the thaumatrope, who is to say that they could not create poetry? Champerret, however, is not content with abstract propositions. Just as Wittgenstein argues that one does not learn a game by reading a book of rules, but by playing it, so, for Champerret, it can be inferred that he believed that practice would prove or disprove the validity of his ideas, which is the point at which he stopped theorizing and began to write poetry using the signs and grids he inherited. Whether he decided on possible meanings for individual signs before embarking on his poetic project, or whether the process of composition itself suggested what these meanings might be, we will never know, but the latter seems the most likely. His notes attaching to each sign show every indication that they were not written all at once, but added to and developed as he worked on the poems. One imagines that in the process of composition, Champerret discovered what the signs *needed* to be, *needed* to mean.

Which leads us, finally, to the poems themselves, which begin to come into clear focus viewed through the lens of the notebooks. The technique is simple, the results startling. Beginning with the proposition that nine signs taken from the cave network, and inserted into the three by three grid, will make a poem, Champerret puts his theory to the test, not by writing one poem, but by writing (if we include his variants) in excess of six hundred. If his hunch is right, he says, then placing signs in the grid will render poems. They are not all *great* poems, but that is beside the point. Not all poems written in English or French in the seventeenth century are great poems, though this is generally considered a rich period for poetic development. That they are poems is indisputable, and Champerret makes his argument by sheer force of numbers. His typical method can be broken into five stages: (i) he fills the grid with signs; (ii) he 'translates' this minimally into French; (iii) he writes through the first translation, adding connector words, so that the poem reads more easily in modern French, translating the three by three structure into stanzaic form, three stanzas of three lines each; (iv) he writes the first variation on the poem, elaborating some of the lines, and embellishing the detail, as a shaman or an oral poet might vary the bare outline of an inherited story; (v) he repeats (iv) continuing to elaborate and embellish the original, as if a different poet were performing the text, all the while maintaining the stanzaic pattern of three stanzas of three lines each, though here the lines are progressively indented to echo the original three by three structure as it is distributed laterally as well as vertically across the page.[6] There is a sixth and final stage sometimes employed, but we will return to that in a moment. Firstly, here is one of Champerret's poems, in its variant translated forms, beginning with stage (i) and proceeding with stages (iii), (iv) and (v) (the signs represent, in order: eye, bison, sun, horns, bison, spears, legs, bison, club):

*

The eye
of the bison
is the sun

the horns
of the bison
are spears

---

6 Champerret left no notes regarding the poetic forms he employed, but in the vast majority of cases (we will look at others later), he employed a form of three stanzas of three lines each. The line is syllabic, and varies from between one and fourteen syllables, tending to increase progressively towards the final stanzaic elaboration.

the legs
of the bison
are clubs

*

The eye
of the bison
is like the bright sun

the horns
of the bison
are like sharp spears

the legs
of the bison
are like heavy clubs

*

The white eye
    of the black bison
        is like a star at night[7]

the curved horns
    of the black bison
        are like sharp spears

the thick legs
    of the black bison
        are like heavy clubs

---

7 Signs for 'sun' and 'star' are interchangeable in Champerret's sign table.

For most poets, this would be enough. More than enough. But Champerret, in what is perhaps his greatest single stroke, revisions the poem one more time by focusing separately on each stanza of his third stanzaic transformation, which he then deconstructs into nine single or multiple word units, then distributes the words across the page, playing freely with line spacing and font size, into three lines of three word units each. These poems are not, as I had first thought on rifling through the Champerret crate, a belated imitation of Mallarmé's poetics as represented in his *Un Coup de dés* of 1896, rather they represent perhaps, in their purity, the only poetry of its time to have understood Mallarmé, and to have taken the tradition that he inaugurated forwards, anticipating, in this respect, the spatialism of Pierre Garnier. In a way that is almost alchemical, Champerret, via the Mallarméan breakthrough, succeeds in refracting his multiply-performed poem through the poetic technology of modernity, and returning it, paradoxically, to its original three by three grid-like structure. Scientifically, this proves nothing, poetically it is a *tour de force*. The work, like Mallarmé's *Un Coup de dés*, is to be read simultaneously across two pages, which cannot be reproduced here, but I refer the reader to the latter pages of this volume where a selection of these poems have been translated into English.

Finally, a further word should be said about Champerret's *Carnet Bleu*, where he begins to experiment with the other grids which he found at Lascaux, realising, perhaps late in the day, that these too could be the basis of poetic composition. As well as the ubiquitous three by three grids, here Champerret draws our attention to other forms of grid structure: single squares, where a single sign could be inserted; squares divided by a vertical line where two signs could be inserted; squares divided by two vertical lines and one horizontal line, where six signs could be inserted; and four by four grids, where sixteen signs could be inserted, among others. Experimenting with these grids, Champerret was able to compose both shorter works – departing from a single sign – and longer narrative structures, taking him to the heart of Ice Age myths. The monostichs, narrative poems, and formally experimental poems that Champerret composed in the *Carnet Bleu*, as well as related compositions on loose leaves (*Feuilles Détachées* as they are called in the archives of the Pôle de la Préhistoire) are here represented in selections from the *Boîte Rouge* where the *Carnet Bleu* and the related *Feuilles Détachées* are archived.

Whether my reading of the jumbled notes in Champerret's notebooks is correct in every detail I cannot say. But in its broad outline it is certainly what Champerret recorded and advanced. Unfortunately, Champerret himself has not left us a lengthy and closely argued dissertation advancing his theories, the thoughts that underpin them, the details and times of his access to the cave network, and how his thoughts might have been refined and taken forward. In one of the letters contained in the crate there is a tantalising indication that Champerret did indeed compose such a document but, alas, it is now almost certainly lost. The letter is from the *Directeur du Musée de L'Homme*, Paul Rivet, and dated June 1941. It is short, so I quote it in its entirety, in the translation by Yves Christophe Lécroart of the Pôle de la Préhistoire:

Dear Sir,

Thank you for your essay on the caves at Lascaux and the mysterious signs therein. We have received a great deal of correspondence regarding Lascaux since its discovery in September 1940, and unfortunately it is not possible to respond to every enquiry in detail. The study of Upper Paleolithic parietal art is a science, and should be left in the hands of specialists, as interference by amateurs can only cause damage to this sacred national inheritance in the long term. Your work is pure fantasy. The signs you describe bear no resemblance to those that have been discovered at Lascaux, and meticulously recorded in tracings and documented in detail by the Abbé Breuil, as outlined in his report presented to the *Académie des Inscriptions et des Belles Lettres* in October 1940.

I sincerely discourage you from pursuing your speculations, and advise you at this moment of national turpitude, to direct your not inconsiderable energies elsewhere.

Yours sincerely

Paul Rivet

Whether or not Rivet read Champerret's essay closely, or at all, we will never know, though his perception of discrepancies between Champerret's collection of signs and those at Lascaux is not without foundation.[8] What is certain is that

---

8   That there are discrepancies between Champerret's signs and those at Lascaux today is beyond question. These are twofold: some signs present in Lascaux are missing from Champerret; while some signs in Champerret do not appear to be present at Lascaux. This said, the overall consonance, given what must have been the brevity of Champerret's visit, or visits, is remarkable. There are several possible explanations for the apparent disparities: (i) that some of the signs noted down by Champerret (those not visible in Lascaux today) rapidly deteriorated as the cave was exposed to air and light and carbon dioxide; (ii) that the light source used by Champerret in the cave created shadow effects which caused Champerret to see signs where there were none; (iii) that

Rivet had other things on his mind, for in June 1940, along with librarian Yvonne Oddon and the Russian ethnologist Anatole Lewitsky, Rivet was establishing a Resistance network operating out of the *Musée de L'Homme*, to oppose the Vichy regime and Nazism. Indeed, the subtext to his letter clearly urges Champerret to get involved with the Resistance himself (Rivet was not to know that he was already deeply embroiled in Resistance activity, and that, ironically, the Lascaux essay and the Resistance work were always already intertwined on

---

Champerret's overactive and overstimulated imagination itself caused him to see signs in the cave's rock surface where they were not; (iv) that Champerret made some of the signs up, speculating, not without reason, that there were likely to be other signs buried beneath the parietal art and the layer of calcite which covered the cave walls in places; and (v) which would account for the signs present in Lascaux but not in Champerret, that Champerret, inevitably, missed some of the signs. This being said, in the history of cave art, there have always been disagreements concerning what is there and what is not. To take the example of Cresswell Crags, the only example of parietal engraving in Britain, whereas Spanish archaeologists Sergio Ripoll, an experienced expert in Ice Age art, and Francisco Muñoz, claimed to have identified upwards of 215 engravings in the Church Hole cave, Paul Pettitt, from the University of Sheffield, and Paul Bahn, have argued that there are only 25 indisputable engraved figures. What Champerret saw, and recorded in his notes and drawings, may well differ from what can be seen today under modern lighting and in well-lit photographs, and yet, many have testified that what we see when *in* a cave, and what we see in a photograph, are ontologically different. It is a tantalizing thought, that what we have preserved in Champerret's notebooks and drawings is actually much closer to what Paleolithic people themselves might have seen.

more than one level).[9] Whatever Rivet had on his mind, the rebuttal must have hit Champerret hard. And yet, this was not the first time in the chequered history of Upper Paleolithic art that major discoveries had been dismissed out of hand. When Marcelino de Sautuola and his daughter, Maria, discovered the polychrome paintings at Altamira in 1879, members of the archaeological establishment, including the prominent French prehistorian, Émile Cartailhac, were quick to denounce Altamira as a fraud. De Sautuola died in 1888, embittered, bankrupt, and discredited.

It is my hope that this volume, introducing Champerret's work to the general reader – it has been known in specialist circles for some time – will go some way towards setting the record straight. David Lewis-Williams, in his study *The Mind in the Cave*, bemoans the advent of the New Archaeologists, whose striving to make archaeology a strictly scientific discipline based solely on empirical evidence – carbon and pollen dating, for example – closes the door on more speculative methods of enquiry, and thus is unable to tackle many of the most urgent questions surrounding the sociological meanings, resonances and significations of cave

––––––––––––

9 In reference to the Nazi occupation of France, it might be added that in this context Champerret's apparently nostalgic verse of *Chants de la Dordogne* could be seen as a mode of resistance in itself, in that it records traditional aspects of French rural life that were under threat of extinction from the Nazis. At a similar period in Britain, when invasion was still a very real possibility, the Recording Britain project, involving artists such as John Piper, Michael Rothenstein, Barbara Jones and Stanley Badmin, was established to record in watercolour and drawing a visual record of people, buildings, landscapes and livelihoods similarly under threat.

art in its more esoteric and ritualistic dimensions.[10] While
Lewis-Williams is not directly concerned with the signs in the
caves, and their specific significations, his arguments indirectly
suggest why Champerret's poetic approach might be valid.
Only by bringing the poetic imagination to bear on the
mysterious signs and marks left by our ancestors on the walls
of the cavern at Lascaux, is Champerret able to restore to us
the lost archive of Ice Age poetry. Champerret's solving of this
great puzzle, like the cracking of a Gestapo code, is achieved
only in and through the poetic imagination. His work, in this
sense, represents a threefold victory for poetry: it is poetry,
here utilised as sacred methodology, that cracks the code; it
is the poetic corpus of *Homo sapiens fossilis* that is thereby
restored to us; and in his own poems, Champerret presents
us with some of the most revolutionary post-Mallarméan
poetry to have been written in the twentieth century. Taken
in its entirety, Champerret's work amounts to no less than the
greatest modern 'defence' of poetry that we have.

Philip Terry, Wivenhoe, 12 September 2021

---

10 See David Lewis-Williams *The Mind in the Cave* (London: Thames
and Hudson, 2002), p. 65.

(BN.CN.01)

watchman	hut	spear
eye	tree	tree
eye	mist	mountains

*

The watchman
by the hut
holds his spear

one eye
on the
trees

one eye
on the mist
the mountains

*

The watchman sits
by the hut
holding his spear erect

he keeps one eye
on the
trees

one eye
on the mist covered
mountains

*

The watchman sits
    motionless by the hut
        clutching [?] his spear tight

he keeps one eye trained
    on the swaying trees
        at the forest's edge

the other eye watches
    the mist as it rises
        over the [mountains]

paw print	crossing	waterfall
paw print	hunters	cave
trap	eye	spears

*

Paw prints at
the crossing by
the waterfall

the paw prints
lead the hunters
to a [cave]

they set the trap
watch
spears ready

*

A line of paw prints
sunk in mud at the crossing
by the waterfall

the hunters
follow the marks
to the [mouth] of a cave

outside they set a trap
and watch
spears at the ready

*

By the crossing
    that leads to the waterfall
        fresh animal prints sunk in mud

following the trail [?]
    hunters trace the paw prints
       to the mouth of a cave

outside they set a trap
    they sit back and watch
       [spears at the ready]

bison   mountains   crossing
bison   mountains   huts
huts   bison   mountains

*

Bison
from the mountains
come to the crossing

bison from
over [?] the mountains
smashing our huts

the huts crushed
beneath the bison
[from the mountains]

*

Bison came
from the mountains
stampeding over the river crossing

a herd of bison
from over the mountains
smashing our huts

our huts crushed
one after the other by the herd
who fell on them like mountains

*

A herd of bison
    came down from the mountains
        leaping and dancing over the crossing

they charged down from the mountains
    a herd of black bison
        smashing our huts beneath heavy hooves

our huts were flattened our mothers
    crushed by the herd of ~~bison~~
        who fell on us like mountains

faces	trees	birdsong
bird	bird	mountains
night	faces	dance

*

Faces
in the trees
not birdsong

the birds
have flown
[to the] mountains

at night
faces
dance

*

Faces move
among the trees
there is no birdsong

winter is coming
the birds are flying
to the mountains

at night singing
the faces dance
in the moonlight

*

Faces silhouetted
    among tall trees
        there is no birdsong to be heard

winter is coming
    the birds are leaving their nests
        flying off over the mountains

at night singing
    the strange faces of the tree spirits [?] dance
        silhouetted in the moonlight

woman   needle   hand
needle   beads   eyes
woman   knot   necklace

*

The woman
holds a needle
in her hand

she takes the needle
and pushes it through
the beads' eyes

the woman makes
a knot
holds up a necklace

*

The woman is holding
a needle carefully
in her hand

moving the needle slowly
she threads it through the eyes
of a row of beads

holding them up
she ties a knot in the gut string
tries on the new necklace

*

The woman is holding
   a bone needle carefully
      between her finger and thumb

moving the needle swiftly
   she threads it through the eyes
      of a line of amber beads

she holds them up
   and ties a knot in the gut string
      shows her new necklace to her companions [?]

footprints	people	river
mist	silhouetttes	spears
eye	trees	fire

*

Footprints
of strangers
by the river

out of the mist
their silhouettes appear
carrying spears

we watch them
from behind the trees
fire in our hearts

*

Footprints in the mud
of others
by the bank of the river

we see their silhouettes
emerge from mist
carrying long spears

we crouch behind the trees
watching them
burning inside

*

By the bank of the river
    there are footprints in the mud
        footprints of tribesmen from beyond the mountains

suddenly we see their forms
    appear out of the grey mist
        carrying their long bone tipped spears

we crouch behind the cover of the trees
    watching their every step
        burning inside with fear

mammoth	mammoth	mammoth
people	hut	hut
axe	spears	river

*

The mammoths
have
arrived

people
gather
outside the huts

with axes and
spears we make our way
down river

*

A herd of mammoth
have arrived
in the plain

the people of the tribe
muster
outside the huts

armed with axes and
tall spears we make
our way down the river valley

*

A herd of woolly mammoth
    have arrived
        crashing into the open plain

the people of the tribe
    muster hurriedly
        outside the hide covered huts

armed with heavy [?] axes
    and tall bone tipped [spears] we tread
        the track down the river valley

mammoth	crossing	night
axe	mammoth	spears
spear	mammoth	forest

*

A single mammoth
by the crossing
at night

we surround it
holding our axes
our spears

when we throw a single spear
the mammoth runs off
into the forest

*

A lone mammoth
is grazing by the crossing
as night falls

we surround it
waving our axes
and spears shouting

when the first spear is thrown
the mammoth ~~cries out~~
running off into the forest

*

An isolated mammoth
    is grazing by the river crossing
        as night begins to fall

we run swiftly towards it
    from all sides waving our axes
        brandishing our spears and shouting

when the first spear is launched
    the mammoth bellows
        charging off into the ~~depths of the~~ forest

			people	wood	cave
			wood	people	scaffold
			eyes	shaman	scaffold
			cave	people	bison
			cave	people	bull
			cave	people	stag
			night	fire	fire
			people	fire	dance
			shaman	dance	antlers

*

People carry
wood
into the cave

with the wood
the people
make a scaffold

under the
eyes of the
shaman

in the cave
the people
paint bison

in the cave
the people
paint a bull

in the cave
they
paint a stag

at night
fires
are lit

the people
gather round the fire
and dance

the shaman too
dances
wearing antlers

*

The tribesmen
carry wood into
the depths of the cave

they are using
the wood to build
a great scaffold

as the tribesmen
tie the trunks with thick
rope the shaman watches

in the dark of the cave
the tribesmen
paint bison

in the dark of the cave
the tribesmen
paint a bull

in the dark of the cave
they
paint a stag

when night falls
many fires
are lit

the people of the village
all gather round the flames
and dance

in the centre the shaman
too dances wearing
antlers on his head

*

The tribesmen
    carry birch trunks into
        the depths of the cave

they are using the
stripped birch to build
    a great scaffold

        under the watchful eyes
    of the shaman they
tie the wood [with thick ropes]

    in the dark cave
        lit by lamps the tribesmen
    paint great bison

in the dark cave
    amidst smoke the tribesmen
        paint aurochs rutting

    in the dark cave
among shadows they
    paint stags swimming through a river

        when night descends
    the villagers light
fires outside the huts

    all together they gather
        round the fires and dance
    late into the night

in the firelight the shaman
    too dances wildly wearing
        on his head a wrack of antlers

eye   bison   sun
horns   bison   spears
legs   bison   club

*

The eye
of the bison
is the sun

the horns
of the bison
are spears

the legs
of the bison
are clubs

*

The eye
of the bison
is like the bright sun

the horns
of the bison
are like sharp spears

47

the legs
of the bison
are like heavy clubs

*

The white eye
    of the black bison
        is like a star at night

the curved horns
    of the black bison
        are like sharp spears

the thick legs
    of the black bison
        are like heavy clubs

woman	comb	hair
night	hunters	forest
ear	night	bird

*

A woman
combs
her hair

it is night
the hunters are
in the forest

she listens
and hears the night
birds

*

A woman sits
combing her
long hair

night has fallen
and the hunting party
is still in the forest

she listens
and hears only the song
of the night owl

*

A woman sits alone
    methodically combing her
        long fine hair

night has long fallen
    and the morning hunting party
        have not returned from the forest

she listens out
    but hears only the sad song
        of the night owl

tooth	fruit	hut
man	tooth	root
tooth	fruit	happiness

*

Eaten
the fruit
in the hut

you will
have to eat
a root

eating
the fruit
happiness

*

I have eaten
the fruit
kept in the hut

you will have to
make do
with roots

eating the fruit
I thought
how delicious

*

To say I have eaten
        the fruit that
                you were keeping in the hut

you will have to
        make do with
                roots when you break fast

eating the fruit
        I thought
                how delicious how cold

light	sun	night
birdsong	birdsong	waterfall
track	river	mountains

*

The light
of the sun
before night

the song
of the birds
by the waterfall

the track
by the river
leading to the mountain

*

A shaft of light
as the sun goes
down at night

the bright song
of the birds
by the waterfall

the track
following the river
winds into the hills

*

The vault of light
    as the sun goes
        down before nightfall

suffused by the song
    of the birds
        by the waterfall's torrent

the twisting track
    following the river
        winds into the distance

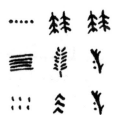

track	trees	trees
shade	leaf	root
people	mountains	root

*

The track
lined
by trees

in the shade
of their leaves
roots grow

people travel
into the mountains
for the roots

*

On the track
sheltered by
a line of trees

beneath the shade
of their leaves
grow edible roots

many people spend
the day on the mountains
to hunt them out

*

On the narrow track
    sheltered by a line
        of black oaks

in the secrecy of their shade
    under the canopy of leaves
        grow the luscious roots

all day in the hills
    people forage on hands and knees
        to find them

antler	stag	forest
eye	stag	star
call	stag	needle

*

The antlers
of the stag
are like the forest

the eye
of the stag
is like a star

the call
of the stag
is like a needle

*

The mighty antlers
of the stag
are like a dark forest

the bright eye
of the stag
is like a star at night

the whistle
of the stag
is like a sharp needle

*

The wrack of antlers
    on the stag's head
        is like a dark forest

the luminous eye
    of the stag [as it turns]
        is like a bright star at night

the piercing whistle
    of the stag [as it falls]
        is like a sharp needle of bone

deer	deer	river
antlers	water	trees
eyes	bush	spears

*

A herd of deer
are crossing
the river

their antlers
above the water
like trees

we watch
from the bushes
spears raised

*

A herd of deer
are swimming over
the river crossing

their black antlers
rise above the water
like a moving forest

we watch in silence
from amidst the bushes
our tall spears raised

*

A vast herd of deer
        are swimming across
                the angry river

their black antlers
        rise out of the water
                like a burnt forest on the move

we watch in silence and fear
        from the shelter of the bushes
                our spears at the ready

branch	hair	forest track
feet	fork	feather
ear	birdsong	birdsong

*

Branches catch
in our hair
on the forest track

beneath our feet
at a fork in the track
feathers

we listen
for the song
of the birds

*

Sharp branches catch
in our hair
on the track through the forest

beneath our feet
where the track divides
there are feathers

we stop and listen
for the call of the birds
in the ~~distance~~

*

Sharp red thorns catch
    in our tangled hair
        on the track through the forest

beneath our feet
    where the track divides
        there are white feathers

we stop and listen in silence
    for the birds
        to begin [?] their singing

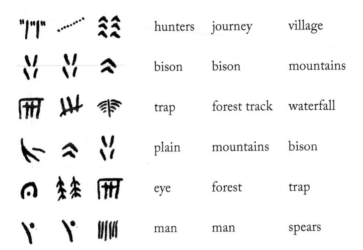

			hunters	journey	village
			bison	bison	mountains
			trap	forest track	waterfall
			plain	mountains	bison
			eye	forest	trap
			man	man	spears

*

The hunters
have returned
to the village

they have found
a herd of bison
beyond the mountains

with our traps
we take the forest track
past the waterfall

in the river valley
over the mountains
the bison graze

we watch them
from the forest
with our traps

the men
stand ready
with spears

*

The hunting party
has returned empty handed
to the village

they have located
a herd of bison
beyond the mountains

armed with our traps
we take the winding track
leading past the bright waterfall into the forest

in the river valley
over the wooded mountains
the bison are grazing

we watch them in silence
from the forest's edge
as we prepare our traps

the painted hunters
stand at the ready
clutching their spears

*

Empty handed the overnight
    hunting party has returned
        to the quiet village

    they have sighted
a herd of red bison
    beyond the black mountains

        armed with our wooden traps
    we take the winding track
up to the bright waterfall and into the forest

    in the flat river valley
        over the black mountains
    the red bison are grazing

we watch them in silence and awe
    from the edge of the forest
        as we prepare our wooden traps

    the brightly painted hunters
stand ready to charge
    clutching their flint tipped spears

eye	night	flute
night	star	star
bird call	night	trees

*

Awake
at night
I play the flute

the night
is filled
with stars

a bird calls
in the night
from the trees

*

Being awake
at night
I rise to play the flute

the night sky
is filled
with a thousand stars

a bird calls
out of the darkness
from the silent wood

*

Being sleepless at
        midnight I rise
                to play my flute

the clear night sky
        is filled with a thousand
                stars gazing at me

a lonely bird
        calls out in the darkness
                from the heart of the wood

eye	star	night
bird	night	flute
night	hut	birdsong

*

I see
not a single star
in the night

birds fly
in the night
as I play my flute

---

11 Another variant of this grid, scribbled at the bottom of the same page in the *Carnet Noir*, has 'eye' under erasure. While such erasures are common in Champerret's notebooks, and frequently indicate doubts or second thoughts, it is tempting to think that here it might signify the negative ie. 'not see' rather than 'see' which would seem to be borne out in Champerret's reading of the poem here, the erasure thereby functioning as a sort of diacritical sign. This possible interpretation is pursued in a paper published in 2020 by Jean-Christophe Poucet, '*Les signes sous-rature de Jean-Luc Champerret*', in *Bulletin préhistorique de la Dordogne* n° 12/2020, pp. 19-39.

it is dark
over my hut
as the birds sing

*

I do not see
my star
in the night sky

birds fly
in the night air
as I play my flute

the darkness hangs
over my hut
as the birds sing

*

I do not see
   my bright star
      in the night sky

majestic cranes fly
   through the night air
      as I blow on my flute

darkness hangs over my hut
   like a perforated shroud
      as the calling cranes [?] fly to the hills

hut	star	star
spears	night	mountains
eye	star	mother

*

Outside the hut
the stars
are shining

like spears
in the night
over the mountains

I watch
the stars
thinking of my mother

*

Outside the lonely hut
the stars are shining
in the night sky

like bright spears
in the darkness
beyond the mountains

I gaze up
at the stars
dreaming of my mother

*

Outside the lonely hut
    the bright stars are shining
        in the night sky

like so many glinting spears
    piercing the darkness
        over the black mountains

I gaze out at the shining
    stars thinking of my mother
        dreaming I am home

hunters	antlers	antlers
antlers	fire	bone straightener
antlers	stick	spears

*

The hunters arrive
carrying
antlers

they put the antlers
in the fire
holding their bone straighteners

fasten the antlers
to sticks
making spears

*

The hunters arrive
carrying armfuls
of antlers

they hold the antlers
in the hot fire
rotating their bone straighteners

they fasten the straightened antlers
to long sticks
making many spears

*

The hunting party returns
    weighed down with armfuls
        of reindeer antlers

they rotate the antlers slowly
    in the hot embers of the fire
        working them with bone straighteners

fasten the straightened antlers
    to long sticks with reindeer gut
        making their sharp spears

pelt	sun	sun
pelt	peg	peg
sun	pot	fire

*

We have put out
the pelts to dry
in the sun

fixing the pelts
with
pegs

as the sun beats down
we stir the cooking pot
by the fire

*

We have stretched out
the reindeer pelts to dry
in the heat of the sun

fixing them in the earth
with strong
wooden pegs

as the sun beats down
we stir the cooking pot
by the hot fire

*

We have stretched out
    the new reindeer pelts to dry
        in the heat of the midday sun

fixing them into the dark
    earth with strong
        wooden pegs

as the hot sun beats down
    we take turns to stir the cooking pot
        feeding it with fire stones

eye	bull	dance
eye	bison	dance
eye	aurochs	dance

*

The eyes
of the bull
are dancing

the eyes
of the bison
are dancing

the eyes
of the aurochs
are dancing

*

The shining eyes
of the bull
start to dance

the dark eyes
of the bison
start to dance

the bright eyes
of the aurochs
start to dance

*

The shining eyes
    of the black bull
        are dancing in the dark

the piercing eyes
    of the red bison
        are dancing in the dark

the bright eyes
    of the great aurochs
        are dancing in the dark

fish   fish   river
bird   bird   river
deer   deer   river

*

The fish
are swimming
in the river

birds
are feeding
by the river

deer
are splashing
in the river

*

The salmon
are swimming
up the river

the birds
are feeding again
by the riverbank

the red deer
are splashing
in the waters

*

The bright salmon
    are swimming and leaping
       in the torrent

the wading birds
    are feeding on the mudflats
       with their long beaks

the red deer
    are splashing and playing
       in the ~~bright~~ water

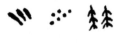

bear	dance	forest
rain	rain	mountains
hut	necklace	dance

*

The bears
are dancing
in the forest

the rain
has come from
over the mountains

in my hut
I put on my necklace
for the dance

*

The cave bears
begin their dance
in the forest

the rain has come
at last from over
the dark mountains

in my hut
I put on my bone necklace
ready for the dance

*

The cave bears
     begin their ~~eupeptic~~ dance
          in the depths of the forest

the spring rains
     have arrived from
          over the black mountains

in the silence of my hut
     I put on my bear tooth necklace
          and prepare for the dance

call	birds	trees
call	deer	plain
call	bear	mountains

*

The call
of the birds
fills the trees

the call
of the deer
fills the plain

the call
of the bear
fills the mountains

*

The bright call
of the birds
fills the trees

the bellow
of the reindeer
fills the river valley

the roar
of the great bears
resounds in the mountains

*

The shrill song
    of the birds
        fills the swaying trees

the hoarse bellow
    of the red deer
        echoes in the river valley

the rasping roar
    of the cave bears
        fills the black mountains

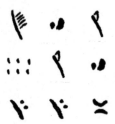

shaman	burial site	torch
people	torch	burial site
woman	woman	song

*

The shaman is going
to the burial site
carrying his torch

the people follow
holding torches
go towards the burial

the women
gather round
singing

*

The shaman advances
towards the burial site
carrying his flaming torch

the villagers follow
likewise holding torches
making their way behind him

the women of the tribe
gather round the stones
chanting their song

*

The shaman advances in short swaying
    steps towards the burial site
        chanting and waving his ceremonial torch

the villagers follow in procession
    holding their flaming brands aloft
        making their way to the burial

the women of the tribe
    gather round the great stones
        chanting their mournful song

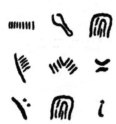

people	lamp	cave
shaman	head dress	chant
girl	cave	mother

*

The people
go with lamps
into the cave

the shaman
is wearing his head dress
chanting

the girl
enters the cave
with her mother

*

The people of the village
go with lamps
into the cave's darkness

the shaman is dancing
antlers on his head
singing the song of the darkness

a young girl
enters the dark of the cave
hand in hand with her mother

*

The elders of the village
    go with grease lamps
        into the vault of the cave's darkness

the shaman begins his dance
    a wrack of antlers tilting on his head
        chanting in tongues

a mother leads her
    virgin daughter [into the cave]
        clutching her tightly by the hand

black	forest	night
black	eye	aurochs
black	black	cave

*

Black is
the forest
at night

black is
the eye
of the aurochs

blacker still
is the
cave

*

Black is the
centre of the forest
in the night

black is the
shining eye
of the aurochs

blacker still is
the cave's
dark heart

*

Black is the
heart of the pine forest
at midnight

black too is
the luminous eye
of the great aurochs

blacker still is
the dark heart
of the painted cave

stag	eye	trees
hut	song	root
stag	trap	journey

*

A single stag
visible
among the trees

in the hut
full of song
roots are eaten

the stag we thought
we had trapped
begins its journey

*

A lone stag
visible
among pine trees

in the noisy hut
full of song
roots are passed round

the stag we thought
we had caught in our trap
begins a new journey

*

A lone stag
    among the pine trees
        turns its [head] and vanishes

in the noisy hut
    full of song and chatter [?]
        roots are passed round as night falls

the stag we thought
    we had caught in our ~~spiked~~ trap
        suddenly breaks free

night	journey	mountains
woman	track	hut
song	rain	trees

*

At night
I came down
from the mountains

a woman
led me
to her hut

we sang
as rain fell
among trees

*

At dusk
I came down
from blue mountains

you
led me
to your busy hut

we sang and drank
as the rain fell
on the pines

*

As dusk fell
    I came down from the mountains
        blue below [?] the skyline

you took my hand
    and led me to your hut
        full of the voices of children

we sang and drank
    rejoicing as the rain came down
        over the dark pines

(BR.FD.01)

Once there were only the black [bears] and the red reindeer on the earth. The black bears spent all their time in the dark of the pine forests, living off honey and insects. The red reindeer spent all their time on the rolling plain, grazing on the long grass and the spiky young leaves of the ~~juniper~~ bushes. Then one day the bears, who had been watching the reindeer from the forest's borders, came down from the dark forest to see what it was like where the reindeer lived. And so the bears and the reindeer began to live side by side on the plain, playing together by the river and in and out of the bushes and running round the great boulders which lay strewn across the valley. And as they continued to live together, playing by the river and in and out of the bushes and running round the great boulders which lay strewn across the valley, bit by bit, the strength of the bear, its might and its woolly coat, mingled with the defences of the reindeer, its great wrack of antlers and its speed over the ground, to make a new creature, the mammoth, which was part like the bear, part like the reindeer, and part like the great boulders round which they loved to play.

---

12 In the *Feuilles Détachées* archived in the *Boîte Rouge* there are a number of prose narratives, of which this is one, which are expanded versions of poems contained in the *Carnet Bleu*. These prose narratives offer an additional variant on the already multiple variants which constitute these narrative poems. Where Champerret has left a prose version of these narratives – given that it is the final development of the narrative and can therefore be considered the definitive version without reasonable doubt – this is the form that has been reprinted here. See also below, *Boîte Rouge: Feuilles Détachées* (B), (C), (D) and (E). The reader wishing to study the variants which precede the prose version can consult them in the manuscripts held in the Pôle de la Préhistoire, Les Eyzies, in the *Boîte Rouge*.

FROM *BOÎTE JAUNE: FEUILLES DÉTACHÉES* (1-3)

The

white

of   the

BLACK

is LIKE

a star

EYE

BISON

at NIGHT

the   CURVED

of the

black

are like

sharp

horns

BISON

SPEARS

the

THICK LEGS

BISON

are

like

of the   black

HEAVY CLUBS

FROM *BOÎTE ROUGE: CARNET BLEU* (A)[13]

(BR.CB.039-044)

The black bulls
have
gathered
on the mountain peaks

the red horses
have
gathered
on the wide plain

---

13 Scattered throughout the *Carnet Bleu* are a number of narrative poems, typically working with a serial four by four grid structure. The different parts of the narrative are not always written sequentially in the notebook, and where this is the case they have been brought together in the most plausible sequence. As with Champerret's other poems, each grid is interpreted in multiple variant ways, yet while with the shorter poems it makes sense to present all variants where space allows, with the narrative sequences, the sense of development of the narrative is lost when all the variants are read side by side. In the interests of preserving the narrative flow, these poems from the *Carnet Bleu* are not presented in their variant forms, rather one variant from each section has been selected. Where the variant selected is the initial word grid, Champerret's habit of presenting these words without breaks between words, adopted throughout the *Carnet Bleu*, has been maintained. Signs, generally left out of the *Carnet Bleu*, are omitted. Readers wishing to consult the full range of variants can find them in the manuscripts held at the Pôle de la Préhistoire in Les Eyzies, in the *Boîte Rouge*.

the screeching birds
have
gathered
in the stormy sky

the dark night of the war
between the bulls
and the horses
is about to begin

*

hornsspearsbullmountains
hoovesclubbullmountains
eyefirebullmountains
callthunderbullforest

*

With their manes | like grass | the horses gather | on the
plain | with their legs | like needles | the horses gather | on
the plain | with their eyes | full of tears | the horses gather |
on the plain | with their eyes | on the mountains | the horses
gather | by the crossing

*

hornsbullhorsehorse
woundwoundwoundwound
hoovesbullhorsehorse
woundwoundwoundwound

*

When the black avalanche
of bull forms bursts onto the wide plain

the horses are mustering at the river crossing
splashing in the muddy water

when the agitated animals
catch sight of the advancing wall of bulls

they panic neighing wildly
scattering in a great arc

the bulls follow hot on their heels
pursuing the frightened beasts through

the red dust clouds rising over the plain
horns lowered to strike

when the horses hit the green wall of the forest's edge
their progress halted by the sharp pines

the bull forms strike them like thunder
skewering them with their deadly horns

*

As far as eyes
can see the
dusty plain is
strewn with the

twitching bodies
of fallen horses
who still let out an
occasional whinny

amongst the
still pines the
contorted bodies
of fallen horses

lie about in
heaps amidst
severed limbs and
gaping eye holes

in the still
flowing river
the limp and
lifeless bodies

of fallen horses
twist and turn
in the current
like strange fish

as night falls
over the river valley
the birds come
and the flies

come to pick
over the still
corpses
of the slain

FROM *BOÎTE ROUGE: CARNET BLEU* (D)[14]

(BR.CB.001)

goatforkgrass
treesbirdsbirdsong

*

A goat stands
at a fork in the track
chewing the grass

in the trees overhead
the birds
sing softly

*

---

14 This section contains a selection of the shorter poems from the *Carnet Bleu* – the longer narrative poems are presented separately (see *Boîte Rouge: Carnet Bleu* A above) – where Champerret experiments with different grids. Due to constraints of space a single variant has been reproduced in each case. Champerret's habit of removing spaces between words in the initial word grid which he adopts throughut the *Carnet Bleu* has been maintained. Signs, likewise, which are on the whole not written out in the *Carnet Bleu*, are omitted. A further selection of these shorter poems from the *Carnet Bleu* is to be found below in the section 'From *Boîte Rouge: Carnet Bleu* (G)'. Readers who wish to consult the full range of variants can find them in the archive held in the Pôle de la Préhistoire in the *Boîte Rouge* (shelf mark: BR.CB.).

(BR.CB.010)

cavejourneystalactitesspider
lampjourneycavewater

*

Going down
into the cave's
darkness
we saw
luminous
stalactites
that sang out
in the dark
we saw
a hairy spider
astride its web

holding our
lamps out
to light the way
we clambered
ever downwards
into the dark
heart of
the cave
following
the sound
of water

*

(BR.CB.024)

footprintbirdsrivercrossing
starskynight

*

The glossy footprints | of the waders | in the mud flats | like
so many stars | spread out | in the night sky

*

(BR.CB.026)

bearbeardanceforest
pawprintpawprinttreestrees
pawprintpawprintskysky
eyesnightskystar

*

The bears | are dancing | in the | forest | they leave | their paw
prints | over | the trees | they leave | their paw prints | over
| the sky | when we look | into the night | sky we see | their
stars

*

(BR.CB.027)

blackblackblackblack
mountainforestplainblack

forestforestfirefire
firefirefirefire
mountainforestplainfire
fireshamanheaddressfire
burningstickforestsky
skyfirefirenight

*

Once there was
    blackness
        everywhere
           and no light

over the mountains
    over the forest
        and over the river valley
           the blackness held sway

then one day which was
    as dark as all other days
        the trees of the forest
           suddenly burst into flame

and as the flames travelled
    from tree to tree
        soon the fire took hold
           until it was everywhere

through the mountains

and through the forest
    and across the river valley
        the fire raged furiously and without end

when everything was burning or burnt
    the shaman stepped out of the mouth
        of the cave and put on his feather
            head dress which gently smouldered

then he stooped down amidst
    the flames picking up a burning
        stick from the forest's edge which
            he hurled into the sky with all his might

so it is that the sun in the sky now
    burns brightly by day
        and the stars in the heavens
            burn brightly by night

*

(BR.CB.035)

shamantoothrivertrees
suntoothcowriver
huntersspearscowpot
shamancowriverbirds

*

The shaman
appears in his
feathered head dress
holding a magic tooth

which he plants in
the soft soil by the banks
of the river beneath
the shade of the pines

on the next day
when the sun rises
the magic tooth
has changed

into a fully grown
black cow
which grazes by
the banks of the river

when the hunters
catch sight of it
they take their
bone tipped spears

and thrust them into
the cow from all sides
carrying the dead meat
off to the cooking pots

after the feasting
at nightfall the shaman

gathers the scattered
bones of the cow and

buries them by the river
where overnight they
metamorphose into birds
which take flight at dawn

*

(BR.CB.036)

deerfork

*

Deer standing motionless at a fork in the track
their antlers barely discernible against the backdrop of trees

*

(BR.CB.045)

thundernight
trackswater

*

Thunder in the night
ripples in the water

*

(BR.CB.055)

deerdeerdeerhorn
spearneedleknifemanstick
mountaindeertrapforest
danceruntrapantlers

*

Once the tall
red deer
carried only
a single

pointed
horn of
bone on
its head

like a sharp
flint tipped spear
a slender
needle of bone

a sharp
blade of flint
a stiff
manstick

then one day
in the black
mountains it so
happened that

out searching
for food the deer

stumbled into a trap
hidden among trees

the deer struggled to
escape from the trap
twisting its head
this way and that

until at last towards
nightfall it broke free
the trap forever stuck on
its head a wrack of antlers

*

(BR.CB.O59)[15]

mothmothjourneyoutofcave
spearknifeaxefire

---

15 This poem is a single minimalist variation from a series of poems by
Champerret where a variety of creatures both real and mythical appear
out of the mouth of a cave and are fought off by the villagers. I have not
included others, as, apart from the change in the identity of the predator,
the poems are almost identical in their verbal stuctures. The creatures
include: spiders, bats, giant tapeworms, demons, and centipedes. In the
most elaborate poem, which begins (in its third variant) 'Giant spiders
emerge/from the dark of the cave/at night' the village shaman is taken
captive by the spiders and imprisoned in the cave in a cocoon, before he
works a spell to turn the spiders to stone. Annie Levallois, of the Pôle de
la Préhistoire, has jokingly referred to this curious sequence of poems as
Champerret's 'B movie' poems, perhaps suggesting that Champerret had
his eyes more on the cinema than on the culture of the Ice Age. And yet,

*

A swarm
of moths

fly out
of the

mouth of
the cave

we fight
them off

with spears
with knives

with axes
with fire

*

---

the proto-cinematic imaginaton of Ice Age artists has been remarked on more than once and is now well documented. They were the inventors of the thaumatrope (see Introduction), and in the Abri du Cap Blanc – no more than a brisk two hour walk from Champerret's birthplace in Le Moustier – the relief sculptures of animals, including horses, bison, and deer, are so arranged that, in a startling anticipation of early cinematic effects, some of the heads appear to move up and down as the light cast by the sun moves through the day's course. Readers wishing to consult the full range of variants can find them in the manuscripts held at the Pôle de la Préhistoire in Les Eyzies, in the *Boîte Rouge*.

(BR.CB.064)

beareyeeyemountains
nightbearbisonplain
nightbearhunterstrap
nightbearflightstar

*

The bear | is the | eye | of the mountain | at night | the bear
dreams | of bison | on the plain | at night | the bear dreams |
of hunters | and traps | at night | the bear dreams | it is flying
| among the stars

*

(BR.CB.065)

birdeyewoman
shamanvoicethunder
birdtearswaterfall

*

A bird | wanted to marry | a woman | the shaman | responded
in a voice | of thunder | the bird | wept many tears | until it
became a waterfall

*

(BR.CB.071)

deerjourneyforest
huntersjourneyhut

*

When the deer
step out of the pine forest
onto the plain

the hunters
come out of their huts
sharpening their spears

*

(BR.CB.078)

birdsflightrivercrossing
horsejourneymountains
deerjourneyforest
bearjourneycave
fishjourneywaterfall
bisonjourneyplain
cowcowmist
spiderjourneyburntforest
catjourneysnow
huntersjourneyspears

*

When the birds
    flock together
        at the narrow river crossing

when the horses
    come down from the mountains
        in a cloud of dust

when the antlered deer
    step out of the forest
        onto the wide plain

when the great bear
    steps out of the mouth of the cave
        into the light

when the leaping fish
    gather
        at the bright waterfall

when the horned bison
    gather
        on the wide plain

when the black cows
    gather together
        in the morning mist

when the hairy black spiders

scuttle out of
    the burning forest of pines

when the big cats
    come out to play
        in the newly fallen snow

the stern faced hunters come
    clutching
        their sharp spears of bone

(BR.FD.03-04)

One day the sun fell out of the sky, coming close to the earth, and began to burn up the pine forest. The sun's heat burnt up all the bushes scattered over the plain. It burnt the feathers off the wings of the birds, so that they tumbled to earth, and it singed all the feathers decorating the shaman's head dress.

The sun burnt up all the water in the river crossing and in the bright waterfall. The sun burnt up all the flowers and the grass on the plain. It burnt the hair off the heads of the young girls, leaving them bald, and it burnt the people's eyes when they looked at it. When the people looked up at the bright sky, all was black. When the people turned their faces to look at the distant mountains, all was black. When the people turned their faces to look out over the wide river valley, all was black. When the people held their hands up to their faces, all was black.

When the people saw nothing but blackness everywhere they looked, they took the narrow path into the heart of the cave to escape the sun's heat. In the darkness of the cave they lit fires to cook tender roots in their cooking pots, they lit fires to roast fat spiders and bats. Then in the darkness of the cave the blind eyes of the people filled with salt tears. The blind eyes of the mothers and the fathers filled with salt tears. The blind eyes of the boys and the girls filled with salt tears. In the cave's darkness even the blind eyes of the shaman filled with salt tears. Then the shaman took his carved stick of bone and gently touched the eyes of all the girls, and the girls danced together round the fire, for they could once more see the light. And the shaman took his carved stick of bone and gently touched the eyes of all the boys, and the boys cried out together beside the fire, for they could once more see the light. In the cave's darkness the blind eyes of the people filled with salt tears. The blind eyes of the mothers and the fathers filled with salt tears. The no longer blind eyes of the boys and the girls filled with salt tears. In the cave's darkness even the blind eyes of the shaman filled with salt tears.

As night fell the boys quietly armed themselves with bone tipped spears and took the sloping path leading out of the cave, past the burial site, to the narrow river crossing. Beneath the bright moon they saw a fallen horse in the river bed. Beneath the bright moon they saw the glowing stars and the burnt forest. Beneath the bright moon they saw the fires burning in the pine trees, they saw the fires burning in the low hills. They saw burnt deer smouldering on the plain, bison burnt to a cinder, and featherless black birds scattered over the ground. The boys searched with their flickering torches amongst the pine trees. They threw their bone tipped spears into the river's narrow channel in the darkness. They returned to the darkness of the cave carrying fish, carrying the feet of a bear, and the burnt carcass of a deer. When the boys got back to the vaulted cave with their catch the shaman put on his scorched head dress and danced wildly round the fire in the flickering darkness. And as he danced round the fire the people began to chant. The boys and the girls chanted, the fathers and the mothers chanted.

On the next night when the boys left the cave to go hunting on the plain the girls took up sharp flints to engrave silhouettes on the wall of the cave. They engraved the silhouettes of a leaping fish and a charging mammoth. They engraved the silhouettes of a great bison and a horned mountain goat. When the boys returned to the darkness of the cave, just as the sun was rising, they came back laden with glistening fish, with the fatty ears of two mammoths, the scorched legs of bison from the plain, and three mountain goats. One night the boys left the darkness of the cave to find soft snow everywhere they looked across the plain. The boys fashioned a great mammoth out of snow. They returned to the darkness of the cave with a handful of berries.

One night soon after it was bitterly cold in the cave, and the frail spirit of the father of the shaman travelled the long road to the bright stars. In his scorched head dress the shaman carried his father to the nearby burial site, where the men and the women chanted solemnly through the cold night. Back in the darkness of the cave the blind eyes of the people filled with salt tears. The blind eyes of the mothers and the fathers filled with salt tears. The no longer blind eyes of the boys and the girls filled with salt tears. And in the cave's darkness the blind eyes of the shaman filled with salt tears.

After this the boys risked going out in the day to hunt for fresh meat. They covered their no longer blind eyes with feathers to protect them from the light of the sun, and entered the pine forest armed with bone tipped spears and clubs. When they returned to the darkness of the cave they came laden with deer and mighty stags. The next day the boys again went out to hunt for fresh meat. Again they covered their no longer blind eyes with feathers to protect them from the light of the sun. Again they entered the pine forest armed with bone tipped spears and clubs, and when they came out of the pine forest they once more carried deer and mighty stags. On the way back it rained heavily and all the feathers covering their eyes fell down on the track. Yet when the boys looked up at the light of the sun everything did not go black. And when the boys held their hands up to their faces everything did not go black. And when the boys looked across the expanse of the plain they saw not blackness, but a rainbow stretched across the sky.

When they got back to the darkness of the cave the blind eyes of the people filled with salt tears. The blind eyes of the mothers and the fathers filled with salt tears. The no longer blind eyes of the boys and girls filled with salt tears. And in the heart of the cave the eyes of the shaman filled with salt tears, as he glimpsed the faint silhouettes of the boys and the girls in the mouth of the cave. As the people cried salt tears the shaman jumped up, putting on his scorched head dress, and danced wildly round the fire in the flickering darkness of the cave. And as he danced round the fire the people began to chant.

The boys and the girls chanted, the fathers and the mothers chanted.

trees	silhouettes	sky
birdsong	birdsong	hills
night	mountains	rain

*

The trees
silhouetted
against the sky

birdsong
in the
hills

at night
among the mountains
rain falls

*

The pine trees
are silhouetted
against the skyline

birdsong
echoes
in the nearby hills

at night
over the distant mountains
rain falls

*

The tall pines
  are silhouetted against
    ~~the~~ luminous sky

the song of birds
  echoes in the darkness
    of ~~the~~ black hills

as night returns
  over the distant mountains
    rain begins to fall

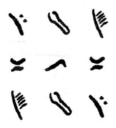

girl	needle	shaman
chant	fire	chant
shaman	needle	girl

*

A girl
carries a needle
to the shaman

people
are chanting
around the fire

the shaman
takes the needle
pricks the girl's arm

*

A young girl
carries the ceremonial needle
to the shaman

the people of the tribe
begin their chanting
around the fire

taking the needle in his hand
the shaman speaks
pricking the girl's arm

*

A young girl carries the
     ceremonial needle of bone to the
          shaman who sits cross legged on the ground

the elders of the tribe
     begin their low chant
          around the scorching embers of the fire

taking the needle between thumb
     and forefinger the shaman speaks the words
          and rises pricking the girl's finger

night   eyes   mountains
hunters   trees   trees
eye   eye   track

*

Night falls
as we look out
over mountains

the hunters
are still out
among the trees

they look everywhere
but see only
the tracks of the stag

*

Night falls
as we look out
over the cold mountains

the late hunters
are still tracking
among the pines

they look all around
but see only
the faint tracks of the stag

*

Night begins to fall
   as we look out anxiously
      over the cold mountains

the belated hunters
   are still busy tracking
      in the forest's dark heart

they search high and low
   but see only the tracks
      of the departed stag

hunters	journey	mountains
eyes	mammoth	bird
eyes	burnt forest	henge

*

The hunters
have returned from their
journey beyond the mountains

they have seen
mammoths and
large birds

they have seen
a burnt forest
and a great henge

*

The hunters have returned
from their long trek
beyond the black mountains

they have seen
woolly mammoths
and great white birds

they have seen
a burnt out forest
and great stones in rows

*

The hunters have returned
        from their long trek into the night
                beyond the black mountains

they have seen many strange things
        herds of woolly mammoth
                and giant white cranes

they have seen many strange things
        a burnt out forest stretching to the earth's end
                and giant stones put there by the gods

people	journey	huts
trees	dance	mist
birds	birds	river

*

The people
have left
their huts

trees
are dancing
in the mist

birds
have returned
to the river

*

The people have left
on a journey
their huts are empty

the trees
weave their shapes
in the mist

flocks of birds
have returned
to the river crossing

*

The villagers have left
    on a long journey
        the huts stand empty

the pine trees
    weave their shapes
        in the morning mist

flocks of white birds
    have returned to the river
        where they gather on the water

rain	rain	mountains
trees	deer	deer
rain	rain	shoot

*

Rain falls
over the
mountains

the trees
are deep
with deer

in the
persistent rain
shoots begin to sprout

*

Rain hangs
over the
black mountains

the pine trees
are deep
with red deer

in the persistent
heavy rain
the shoots begin to sprout

*

Pelts of rain
    hang over the
        distant black mountains

the pine trees
    are deep with reindeer
        that flow like a river

as the persistent
    heavy rain falls down
        the green shoots begin to sprout

man	path	mountains
waterfall	mountains	mountains
girl	man	needle

*

A man
follows the winding path
into the mountains

by the
waterfall
hidden among the peaks

a girl hands
him a
needle

*

The young man
follows the twisting path
that leads to the peaks

by the bright waterfall
hidden among
mountains

the waiting bride
hands him
the needle

*

The chosen man
    follows the winding path
        that leads to the peaks

by the bright waterfall
    concealed among
        the mountain's heights

the waiting bride passes
    the needle of bone
        to her chosen one

girl	necklace	happiness
mountains	mountains	mountains
fire	fire	rain

*

The girl
puts on her necklace
smiling

the
mountains
are unmoved

the fire
must be tended
if it is not to go out

*

The young girl
puts on her new necklace
with a smile

the black mountains
are
unmoved

the burning fire
must be watched
if it is not to go out

*

The young girl
    puts on her necklace of shells
        with a bright smile

the black mountains
    austere and foreboding
        are unmoved

the fire of wood and bone
    must be constantly tended
        if it is not to go out in the rain

eye	cave	needle
black	cave	night
divide	cave	antler

*

The eye
of the cave
is like a needle

the darkness
of the cave
is like the night

the forking
of the cave
is like an antler

*

The winking eye
at the cave's mouth
is like a shining needle

the pitch black
of the cave's heart
is like the dead of night

the secret place
where the cave divides
is like a branching antler

*

The winking black eye
    of the cave's dark [entrance]
        is like the eye of a needle of bone

the impenetrable dark
    of the cave's black heart
        is like a night with no moon

the hidden place
    where the cave divides
        is like the branching of the stag's antler

forest	fire	fire
burning	burning	fog
people	river	eyes

*

The forest
has caught
fire

the burning
has made
a great fog

the people
stand by the river
watching

*

The forest of pines
has caught fire
and is blazing

the angry flames
are spitting a cloud
of blackness into the sky

the frightened villagers
stand by the river crossing
crying shouting watching

*

The dark forest of pines
    has caught fire like dry moss
        it blazes like the sun

the angry flames
    spit clouds of blackness
        making the day night

the dark eyed villagers
    stand trembling by the crowded river crossing
        crying leaping shouting watching

eye   girl   star
eye   mourner   rain
eyes   hunters   spears

*

The eye
of the girl
is like a star

the eye
of the mourner
is like rain

the eyes
of the hunters
are like spears

*

The bright eye
of the young girl
is like a shining star

the dark eye
of the keening woman
is like the falling rain

the sharp eyes
of the hunters
are like pointed spears

*

The bright blue eyes
    of the young girl
        are like stars shining [in the night]

the dark red eye
    of the woman in mourning
        is like the endless ~~falling~~ rain

the vigilant eyes of the hunters
    as they track their prey
        are like flint headed spears

woman	root	pot
eye	root	fire
fire	pot	mist

*

The woman
puts roots
in the cooking pot

she watches
the roots
cooking beside the fire

as she adds the fire stones
the cooking pot breathes
its mist

*

The women of the tribe
put the fresh roots
in the cooking pot

they watch the roots
stirring them gently
as they cook beside the fire

as they drop in the hot fire stones
the cooking pot breathes
its grey mist

*

The old women of the tribe
    put the freshly scrobbed roots
        into the cooking pot

they watch the roots
    stirring them gently from time to time
        as they cook beside the glowing fire

as they drop in the hot fire stones – *plok!* –
    the ~~deer hide~~ cooking pot belches
        breathing its warm grey mist

forest	burning	burning
people	journey	river
journey	waterfall	mountains

*

The forest
is
burning

people
move
across the river

past
the waterfall
into the mountains

*

The forest
has caught fire
screaming in the night

the villagers are afraid
they take what they can carry
and make haste over the river

following the winding track
that leads past the waterfall
and into the mountains

*

The pine trees are all ablaze
    screaming and crackling in the night sky
        filling the air with thick swirling smoke

the tribespeople are frightened
    they take all they can carry
        and splash through the river crossing

clattering up the long and winding track
    that leads past the bright waterfall
        and into the safety of the mountains

woman	eye	root
woman	eye	shoot
woman	eye	herb

*

The women
are looking
for roots

the women
are looking
for shoots

the women
are looking
for herbs

*

The women are out
looking for roots
in the sandy soil

the women are out
looking for shoots
in the dark mud

the women are out
looking for herbs
amidst the grasses

*

The women are out with their deerskin sacks
    looking for tender black roots
        in the sandy soil under the dark oaks

the women are out with their deerskin sacks
    looking for fresh green shoots
        in the dark mud by the swamp

the women are out with their deerskin sacks
    looking for dark scented herbs
        amidst the grasses on the plain

shaman	horns	bison
feather	head dress	river
shaman	journey	night

*

The shaman
has been struck
by the horns of the bison

his feathers
and his head dress
lie by the river

the shaman
is making the long journey
into the night

*

The shaman ~~of the tribe~~
has been struck by
the deadly horns of the bison

his bright feathers
and his head dress of antlers
lie abandoned by the river

we gather his body
and lay him to rest
ready for his death journey

*

Courageous in battle the shaman ~~of the tribe~~
    has been pierced by the
        death bringing horns of the bison

his gay feathers and his great head dress of antlers
    lie abandoned by the river crossing
        amidst the rhinoceros dung

we gather his cold stiff body
    and lay him to rest with spear and totem
        ready for the long journey into the night

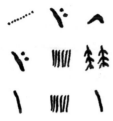

journey	woman	hut
woman	sticks	forest
rope	sticks	rope

*

After the journey
the women
build huts

they take
long sticks
from the forest

and bind them
together
with rope

*

After a long journey
the women of the tribe
are erecting the new huts

they take long birch wood sticks
from the borders of the forest
and fix them [in the earth]

they bind them together
with lengths of rope
cut from the hide of deer

*

After a long journey up river
    all the women of the tribe
        are busy constructing the new huts

they cut the long birch wood sticks
    that grow at the forest's borders
        and fix them in the dark earth

they bind them together with strips
    cut from the hide of the reindeer
        then layer the huts with branches and skins

man	journey	mines
eyes	flint	spears
eyes	flint	axe

*

The men
have gone on a journey
to the mines

they are looking
for flint
for their spears

they are looking
for flint
for their axes

*

The men of the village
have left on a journey
to the flint mines

they are searching
for black flint
for their spear heads

they are searching
for black flint
for their axe heads

*

The men of the village have departed
        making the long journey over the hills
                to the place where the flint lives

when they get there they will search for
        heavy lumps of shining black flint
                to crack open for their spear heads

when they get there [they will search for]
        heavy lumps of shining black flint
                to crack open for their axe heads

girl	girl	fire
mother	needle	pelt
mother	song	needle

*

The girls
have gathered
round the fire

their mothers
show them how to sew
the pelts

their mothers show them
how to sing
as they sew

*

The girls of the tribe
have gathered together
round the great fire

their mothers show them
how to sew the pelts together
with the needles of bone

their mothers show them
how to sing our songs
as they hold the needles

*

The young girls of the tribe
    gather together excitedly
        round the quick flames of the fire

their mothers show them
    how to stitch the reindeer pelts
        with the sharp needles of bone

their mothers show them – *la-la ha-la!* –
    how to sing the songs of the tribe
        as they work the sharp needles of bone

wound	bison	vulva
eye	bison	mother
spear	bison	manstick

*

The wound
in the bison's side
is like a vulva

the eye
of the bison
is like a mother

the spear
in the bison's side
is like a manstick

*

The dark wound
in the bison's flesh
is like an open vulva

the dark eye
of the turning bison
is like a betrayed mother

the long shafted spear
in the bison's side
is like a stiff manstick

*

The dark and gaping wound
    in the bison's torn flesh
        is like an open vulva

the dark and luminous eye
    of the wheeling bison is like
        a betrayed and outraged mother

the long shafted spear
    in the bison's dark hide
        is like a hard and angry manstick

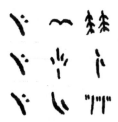

girl	bird	forest
girl	footprint	fork
girl	deer	hunters

*

The girl
is like a bird
in the forest

the girl
is like a footprint
at a fork in the track

the girl
is like a deer
wary of hunters

*

The new girl
is like a white bird
in the forest

the new girl
is like a faint footprint
at a fork in the track

the new girl
is like a frightened deer
wary of approaching hunters

*

The new girl in the village
    is like a white bird
        in the heart of the forest

the new girl in the village
    is like a fading footprint
        in the sand at a fork in the track

the new girl in the village
    is like a frightened deer
        wary of the spears of ~~approaching~~ hunters

			eye	woman	star
			hair	woman	waterfall
			tooth	woman	knife
			legs	woman	fork
			breast	woman	fruit
			vulva	woman	needle

*

The eye
of a woman
is like a star

the hair
of a woman
is like a waterfall

the tooth
of a woman
is like a knife

the legs
of a woman
are like a fork in the track

the breast
of a woman
is like fruit

the vulva
of a woman
is like a needle

*

The glistening eye
of a woman
is like a bright star

the shining hair
of a woman
is like a glimmering waterfall

the sharp tooth
of a woman
is like a bone knife

the slender legs
of a woman are like
an inviting fork in the track

the soft breast
of a woman
is like succulent fresh fruit

the bared vulva
of a woman
is like a needle of bone

*

The dark dilating eye
    of a turning woman
        is like a star enfolded by the night

    the cascading hair
of a woman at sunset is like
    the glimmer of a waterfall in the forest glade

        the sharp bared tooth
    of a woman in anger
is like a hidden knife of bone

    the slender and mischievous legs
        of a woman dancing round a fire
are like an inviting fork in the track

the succulent bare breasts
    of a woman caught in desire
        are like the dark fruit of the forest

    the bare naked vulva
of a woman on heat
    is like a sharp needle of bone

grass	shade	woods
hunters	spears	night
dawn	spear thrower	mountains

*

Grass rustles
in the shade
of the woods

hunters
throw spears
into the night

dawn finds
the spear thrower
in the mountains

*

The grasses rustle
in the shade
of the dark woods

the hopeful hunters
launch their spears
into the night

the light of dawn discloses
the bone spear thrower
lost in the mountains

*

The spring grasses rustle
    beneath the shade
        of the dark oak woods

the expectant hunters
    launch their flint tipped spears
        into the night air

the dim light of dawn discloses
    the carved bone spear thrower
        lost in the rocky heights

footprints	night	hut
star	birds	river
water	eyes	fish

*

Footprints
at night
outside my hut

stars
like birds
fly over the river

beneath the water
the eyes
of fish

*

Footprints from the mountains
left at night
outside my cold hut

flying stars
like white birds
shoot across the river

beneath the surface of the water
the bright eyes
of the fish

*

Footprints of the mountain goat
    left in the darkness
        outside my cold and sleeping hut

bright flying stars
    like great white birds
        pass high over the river

beneath the bubbling surface of the water
    the unblinking eyes
        of the fish

bison	mountains	river crossing
aurochs	reindeer	mammoth
people	hut	eyes

*

The bison have
come down from the mountains
to the river crossing

with the aurochs
the reindeer
and the mammoths

the people
sit in their huts
watching

*

The rutting bison are
charging down the mountain
to the busy river crossing

with the great aurochs
the swimming reindeer
and the woolly mammoths

the people of the village
sit tight in their huts
listening watching

*

The rutting black bison
    are shuffling down the high mountains
        towards the [turbulent] river crossing

great aurochs splash in the waters
    clashing with the antlers of the reindeer
        clashing with the mammoths' mighty tusks

to the last man and woman the people of the village
    sit tight in the safety of their huts
        listening watching scarcely breathing

shaman	fire	flute
man	woman	ear
shaman	flute	people

*

The shaman is
sitting by the fire
playing his flute

the men
and women
listen

the shaman
holds out the flute
to them

*

The shaman is
sitting by the fire
quietly playing his flute of bone

the young men
and women of the village
gather round to listen

he stops
and hands the flute round
for them to have a go

*

With only a single feather in his hair
    the shaman is sitting by the fire
        playing his flute of bone

the young boys and girls
    of the village come out of their huts
        and gather round excitedly to listen

when the shaman has finished his tune
    he puts down his flute and passes it round
        for the children to have a go

shaman	head dress	flute
shaman	dance	fire
people	path	club

*

The shaman
in full head dress
is playing his flute

as he
dances
round the fire

the people
go down the path
with clubs

*

The shaman in full
head dress plays
his flute menacingly

as he dances
ecstatically
round the sacred fire

in procession the villagers
make their way down the path
carrying clubs

*

Bedecked with feathers and in
    full head dress the shaman
        trills menacingly on his flute

as he stamps rhythmically
    round the fire's crackle
        dancing himself into a death trance

in solemn procession the elders
    make their way slowly down the track
        to the sacrifice carrying clubs

shaman	night	hut
head dress	necklace	root
fire	man	woman

*

The shaman
at night
enters his hut

he takes off his head dress
and his necklace
and chews on some roots

he goes to sit by the fire
with the men
and the women

*

The shaman
when it is getting dark
enters his hut and rests

he takes off his heavy head dress
and his shell necklace
and chews on dark roots

later he goes to sit by the fire
chatting with the men
and the women gathered there

*

When night is approaching
    the shaman puts aside his magic
        enters his hut and rests

he takes off his head dress of antlers
    and his noisy necklace of shells
        and sits down to chew on some roots

later he will go and sit by the fire
    chatting quietly with the men and women gathered there
        laughing and playing with the children

rain   night   rain
night   night   rain
rain   rain   rain

*

Rain
all night
rain

all through
the night
rain

rain
rain
rain

*

It is raining
all through the night
non stop rain

without let up
the rain falls
through the night

rain falls
more rain
then more rain

*

It is raining incessantly
    all through the long night
        rain rain rain rain

without let up for an instant
    the hard rain falls through the night
        rain rain rain rain

the rain falls and falls and falls
    more rain and then more rain
        rain rain rain rain

girl	eyes	hut
boy	path	river
shaman	path	head dress

*

A girl
looks out
from her hut

boys
on the path
to the river

the shaman
follows them
wearing his head dress

*

A girl peers out
from the slit
of her hut

boys are gathering along the track
that leads to the river
to begin their washing

behind them the shaman follows
the same track
on his head a wrack of antlers

*

At dawn a girl looks out
    from the shelter
        of her deerskin [?] hut

boys follow the narrow path to the river crossing
    to begin the washing
        that precedes the sacrifice

the shaman follows ~~behind them~~
    with a limping step
        on his head a wrack of antlers

girl	root	pot
eyes	mountains	rain
eyes	root	pot

*

The girl
places the roots
in the pot

she watches
the mountains
where rain gathers

she watches
the roots
in the pot

*

The girl drops
the fresh roots
in the cooking pot

she keeps an eye
on the distant mountains
where rain clouds gather

she watches the roots
in the cooking pot
stirring them now and then

*

The girl places the fresh roots
    in the cooking pot
        adding hot stones from the fire

she watches the distant mountains
    where rain is gathering
        where the thunder god is calling [?]

she watches the roots [in the pot]
    stirring them from time to time
        ~~waiting~~ till they are <u>good to eat</u>

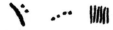

girl	comb	hair
girl	beads	hair
eyes	fire	dance

*

The girl
combs
her hair

she puts
beads
in it

she looks out
at the fire
at the dance

*

The young girl
carefully combs
her long hair

then proceeds
to string it
with coloured beads

she looks out
at the fire
at the people dancing

*

Tilting her head to one side
    the young girl combs
        her long black [?] hair

taking some strands
    between finger and thumb
        she strings them carefully with ~~coloured~~ beads

she looks out at the fire
    watching the people gathering
        singing and dancing round the flames

FROM *BOÎTE JAUNE: FEUILLES DÉTACHÉES* $(4\text{-}6)$

The

winking

CAVE'S

is like the EYE

of a needle

BLACK EYE

of the

dark entrance

of bone

impenetrable

DARK

of the cave's

BLACK

is like   a night

the

HEART

with no moon

the

         hidden
           place

where   the

is like   *the branching*
    of the stag's antler

cave   DIVIDES

FROM *BOÎTE ROUGE: CARNET BLEU* (B) [16]

(BR.CB.046-051)

The solemn mourners gather at the burial site where the body
of the shaman lies dressed in its ceremonial head dress

standing in a ring the mourners sing their low chant
as the body of the shaman is placed on the fire

they watch in silence as the crackling flames
take hold engulfing the shaman's body

just as the sun is sinking they see the luminous
soul of the shaman darting from the flames

just as the sun is sinking they see the luminous
soul of the shaman take flight in bird form

*

When the spirit | of the shaman | takes flight | in bird form
| it alights | in the trees | from where it sings | in the night |
at dawn from its | perch in the trees | it watches | the huts | it
watches | the hunters as | they set off on the | long path to the
mountains

*

The bright spirit
of the shaman is

---

16 A selection. See note to *Boîte Rouge: Carnet Bleu* (A).

singing in the oak trees
at night

unable to sleep the
hunters go to see the bird
perched in the high branches
of the oak

they call out to
the spirit hidden
amongst the leaves –
come down bird come down! –

the bird shifts to a higher branch
calls out in a piercing screech
then takes flight
into the dark of the night

*

spiritflightmountainsbirds
birdsplaineyesspirit
spiritcallairsong
spiritflightbirdsmountains

*

One day the bright
spirit of the
shaman returns
to the village
in his bird

form to
talk to his
people again

in his soft
bird voice
he tells us
stories of his life
in the cold
black mountains
among the feathered
bird people

in his soft
bird voice
he describes to
us what it is like
to fly through the
sun streaked clouds
at dawn on a
winter morning

in his soft bird
voice with sadness
in his eyes he tells
us what it is like
to see your brother
meet his death
flailing helplessly
in a trap

*

On the day the spirit | of the shaman | returns to the huts | to see the people | we take him | down the track | to the burial site | of his mother | he looks | at the grave | with tears | in his eyes | as night falls | he remains fixed to the spot | by morning | he has flown

FROM *BOÎTE ROUGE: FEUILLES DÉTACHÉES* (B)

(BR.FD.02)

Once there were only white birds and black bison on the face of the earth. The white birds spent all their time in the bright sky, flying high up among the clouds, occasionally coming to rest in the pine trees of the forest. The black bison spent all their time on the rolling plain, grazing quietly on the long grass, or buffeting each other with their sharp horns at rutting time. Then one day the birds, who had been watching the bison from high up in the air, came down from the bright sky to see what it was like where the bison lived. And so the birds and the bison began to live side by side on the plain, playing together by the river and in the bushes and chasing each other through the trees. And as they continued to live side by side, playing together by the river and in the bushes and chasing each other through the trees, bit by bit, the strength of the bison, its mighty horns and its powerful legs, mingled with the swiftness of the bird, its darting flight and its alert eye, to make a new creature, the gazelle, which was part like the bird, part like the bison, and like the colour of the wide plain where they loved to play.

FROM *BOÎTE ROUGE: CARNET BLEU* (E)[17]

(BR.CB.003)

river

*

The river

*

The river stretching out across the plain

*

The river stretching out across the plain as far as the eye can
   see

*

(BR.CB.004)

track

*

The track

*

The track winding into the mountains

---

17 This section contains a selection of Champerret's monostichs from
the *Carnet Bleu*. See also *Boîte Rouge: Carnet Bleu* (F) below.

*

The track winding into the mountains to the peaks

*

(BR.CB.005)

deer

*

The deer

*

The deer hiding in the undergrowth

*

The deer hiding in the undergrowth on the path to the
waterfall

*

(BR.CB.006)

bird

*

The bird

*

The bird singing in the pine tree

*

The bird singing in the pine tree at dusk

*

(BR.CB.007)

needle

*

The needle

*

The sharp needle of bone

*

The sharp needle of bone in the fingers of the new bride

*

世 \

goatpost

*

The goat is tied to the post

*

The goat feeds tied to its post

*

The goat must browse where she is tied

*

❦❦

birds

*

The birds are in flight

*

The birds are flying overhead

*

The birds are flying where are they going to?

*

skynecklacefire

*

The sky is a necklace of fire

*

The sky at night is a necklace of fire

*

The sky at night is a shimmering necklace of fire over the
    hills

*

eyegoatneedle

*

The eye of the goat is like a needle

*

The sharp eye of the mountain goat is like a needle of bone

*

The vigilant eyes of the goat on the mountain ridge like
    sharp needles of bone

*

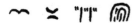 (BR.CB.025)

birdsonghuntersears

*

When the bird sings the hunters listen

*

When the birds sing in the branches hunters are listening at
   the roots

*

When birds herald the spring beware the ears of hunters

*

(BR.CB.028)

spiritenemiesclubfeather

*

If a spirit is your enemy the club will be as a feather

*

If a goddess is your enemy your club will be no more use
   than a feather

*

If the gods are your enemies you may as well go to war with
   feathers

*

(BR.CB.030)

manmanman
potfishfire

*

Many men at the pot fish burn

*

Too many men beside the cooking pot and the fish will burn

*

Too many men round the cooking pot and the fish will spoil

*

(BR.CB.031)

birdhandhand
birdbirdbush

*

A bird in our hands birds in the bushes

*

A bird held in the hands two birds singing in the bushes

*

A bird in the hands is like two in the bushes

*

   (BR.CB.032)

fishfishfishriver

*

There are fish in the river

*

There are many fish in the river

*

There are plenty of fish in the river so what?

*

eyeblackforest
treetreetree

*

The eye is blind to the forest – a tree a tree a tree

*

The eye cannot see the forest – only the trees

*

The eye cannot see the forest for the trees

*

bisonmountainsmany
bisonplainfew

*

The bison over the mountains are many the bison on the
   plain few

*

The herd of bison over the mountains is big the herd of bison
   in the river valley is small

*

The herd of bison grazing over the mountains is always
   bigger than the herd of bison grazing on the plain

FROM *BOÎTE ROUGE: CARNET BLEU* (G)[18]

(BR.CB.098)

starfireforest
starfireriver
starfireheaddress
starfiremammoth
starfiremountains
starfirehuts
starfirebison
starfirefaces
starfirefish
starfirewaterfall
starfirecave
starfiredeer
starfirecat
starfirestar

*

That star
    will incinerate
        the black forest of pines

that star
    will scorch
        the river bed to a cinder

---

18 A selection of poems from the *Carnet Bleu*. See note to *Boîte Rouge: Carnet Bleu* (D).

that star
    will frazzle
        the shaman's feathered head dress

that star
    will desiccate
        the woolly mammoths reducing them to charred
            lumps of flesh

that star
    will melt
        the black mountains into fistfuls of rock

that star
    will ignite
        the wooden huts reducing them to ash

that star
    will fry
        the watery eyes of the black bison

that star
    will cauterise
        the people's faces reducing them to bone

that star
    will combust
        the silver fish as they leap at the waterfall

that star
    will ignite
        the bright waterfall turning it to dust

that star
    will singe
        the mouth of the cave turning it into a death trap

that star
    will turn
        the red deer yellow and stinking

that star
    will sizzle
        the whiskers of the big cats so that they run off in a
            ball of fire

that star
    will explode
        all the other stars creating a conflagration in the sky

*

(BR.CB.099)

rootpot
shamanhorse
shamanwomanhorse
huthorsehorse
nighthunterssongfire
dawnplainhorsehorse

*

When there is nothing but dry black roots
    to put in the empty cooking pot

the shaman dances wildly
    taking the form of a stallion

the shaman's
    woman too dances wildly
        in her horse form

in the darkness of the hut
    they cry out
        making many horses

all night long
    the hunters leap
        round the fire
            singing and chanting

when dawn breaks at last
    the miracle has occurred
        the wide plain is filled
            with stampeding horses

*

(B R . C B . 1 1 5)

shamansacrifice
girlnecklace
huntersspear
watchmannight
boyfish
womanvillage
motherboy

*

The shaman remembers
    the blood at his first sacrifice

the girl remembers
    her first necklace of bright shells

the hunters remember
    their first spear and their first kill

the watchman remembers
    his first sleepless night

the boy remembers
    the first fish he speared in the river

the woman remembers
    the village where she was born

the mother remembers
    her first boy child and how he squealed in the night

*

(BR.CB.117)

peoplepathcaveblack
beartrackstarstar
peopletrackblackcave
eyetorchbearcave

*

The people took | the path leading to | the cave's | darkness |
the bears | had departed | taking the long track | to the stars

| they followed | the track | penetrating the | cave's darkness
| and saw | with the light of a torch | the outline of a bear |
on the cave wall

*

(B R . C B . 1 2 2)

blacksun
sunrain
rainriver
riverfish
fisheye
eyebear
bearstar
starbird
birdfootprint
footprintbison
bisontrap
trapdeer
dearhorse
horsegoat
goatcow
cowspider
spidercave
cavedarkness
darknessfire
firespear
speardeath
deathclub
clubdeath
deathman
mandeath
deathdeath

*

In the beginning was black
    who begat sun

who begat
    rain

who begat
    river

who of course begat
    fish

who begat
    eye

who begat
    bear for bears have eyes

who begat
    star for the bear is in the sky

who begat
    bird

who begat
    footprint for birds leave footprints

who begat
    bison for so do bison

who of course begat
    trap

who begat
   deer

who begat
   horse

who begat
   goat

who begat
   cow

who begat
   spider

who begat
   cave for spiders live in caves

who begat
   darkness

who begat
   fire for fire comes out of darkness

who begat
   spear for spears come out of darkness

who begat
   death

who begat
   club

who begat
    death

who begat
    man

who begat
    death

who begat
    death

*

(BR.CB.134)

rain
rain
rain
rain
rain
rain
rain
rain
rain
rain
rain
rain
rain

*

The rai n
 fall s
  ina n
   endles s
    downpour
   the rai n
    fa l ls
      in an
      endle ss
      s tre am
       d own it falls
       the rain
       d own
       do w n
       d ow n
       d own

        d

          o

            w

            n

FROM *BOÎTE JAUNE: FEUILLES DÉTACHÉES* (7–9)

on the

stag's

BROW

is like

a dark

forest

The wrack

of

antlers

of   the

                    is like

the

luminous

eye

STAG

a bright STAR

at dawn

the

      piercing

          whistle

        of

           the

                        stag

is like

a *SHARP*

hot needle

FROM *BOÎTE JAUNE: CARNET GRIS*[19]

(BJ.CG.01)

*

---

19 In the *Carnet Gris* Champerret took the three by three grids from the *Carnet Noir* and read them not from left to right and top to bottom, but in every other conceivable way, from right to left and bottom to top, right to left and top to bottom and so on. The result is that each poem in the *Carnet Noir* yields seven new poems (as the grids can be read in eight different ways when treated as reversible in this way), or twenty-one new poems if we consider all three variants (the number increases to thirty-five if we include all five stages of Champerret's process). This being the case, while Champerret did not complete the set of possible variants for every grid contained in the *Carnet Noir*, the number of poems generated by this method is vertiginous. We therefore include only a selection of the most typical poems. Champerret's procedure is as follows: poems marked (a) proceed from bottom right, right to left, and bottom to top; poems marked (b) proceed from bottom right, bottom to top by column, and right to left; poems marked (c) proceed from bottom left, bottom to top by column, and left to right; poems marked (d) proceed from top left, top to bottom by column, and left to right; poems marked (e) proceed from bottom left, left to right, and from bottom to top; poems marked

(c)

The eyes | of the | watchman shift | from the mist | to the
trees | to the huts | to the mountains | to the trees | to the
spear which he clutches

*

(e)

The sharp eye | sees mist dancing | the mountain breathing
| the sharp eye | sees a tree talking | to another tree | the
intent watchman | sits in silence | by his hut of spears

*

(f) proceed from top right, top to bottom by column, and right to left;
and poems marked (g) proceed from top right, right to left, and from
top to bottom. Signs in different poems, even in the same sequence, are
sometimes interpreted differently in different poems to fit with the ever-
changing context, therefore the 'interpretation' of the sign, which is fluid,
has not been given here as it has elsewhere. The situation is complicated
further by Chaperret's new practice in the *Carnet Gris* of not only
expanding poems to give multiple variants, but of *reducing* them to create
minimalist variants, sometimes as many as nine per poem. Potentially
this creates an additional sixty-three poems from each source poem from
the *Carnet Noir*, creating a dizzying total of a possible ninety-eight new
poems for each source poem. These minimalist variants are marked (a'),
(b'), (c') etc. Given the number of poems generated by this method, to
save on space, Champerret adopted his frequent method of marking line
breaks with a vertical bar, which we have maintained here. Readers who
wish to see for themselves the poems in all their variants are referred to
the *Carnet Gris* archived in the *Boîte Jaune* at the Pôle de la Préhistoire.

(f)

The sharp pointed spear | is a lone pine tree perched | on the
peak of the mountains | the sleeping hut at dawn | is a ring
of pine trees | in the rising mist | the vigilant watchman |
motionless by his hut | is an eye and an eye

*

(g)

The spear rests | in the hut | of the watchman | the trees |
look back | at him | the mountains | and the mist | look back
at him

*

(BJ.CG.02)

*

(d)

There are paw prints and hoofprints | leading to the trap at
the forest's edge | whatever is in there cannot get out | from
the safety of the river bank | the hunters can see them carved
in the dark earth | leading to the trap's open mouth | they

move swiftly and silently past the bright | waterfall past the
dark mouth of the cave | clutching their raised spears tightly

*

(f)

Behind the waterfall the cave | behind the cave's mouth | the
hunters sharpen their spears | spread out across the river | the
hunters peer into the water | looking for fish | there are no paw
prints | to follow just the waiting | as the fish swim into the trap

*

(g)

Beneath the waterfall | by the crossing | a paw print | in the
cave | the hunters | do not see it | in the dark their spears |
and eyes are useless | the cave a trap

*

(BJ.CG.03)

*

(a)

A trail of footprints | by the river turns our faces | towards the water | suddenly the whole village | is like a flock of birds | in flight | our plaintive chant | the chant of the tribe | fills the forest

*

(b)

Footprints criss cross | the village in haste | as the slow chant begins | across the forest | the faces of birds and beasts | take flight | in the water | the bird people | begin their dance

*

(d)

The people are watching the | mustering birds with curiosity | as they drop down into the water | standing at the edge of the forest | the dream of flight is clearly | marked on their bright faces | later a shrill chant imitating | the song of birds sounds out from the forest | a single line of footprints leads to the cliff

*

(e)

Beneath the surface of the water | drowned faces peer out | bearing the marks of heavy footprints | the birds have taken flight | swirling in dark clouds | above the deserted village

| the people of the tribe | are gathered in the forest | where they make their low chant

*

(f)[20]

There is frenzied chanting | in the village | footprints of captives trail into the hills | the pine forest is awake | with the flight | of fear struck faces | both people and birds | have abandoned the | shallow river crossing

*

(g)

The chanting of | the forest people | began at dawn | the village | took flight | with the birds | leaving footprints | and faeces | by the water

*

---

20 This poem, with its sinister reference to captives being led off into the hills, given the historical context of the compositions, cannot fail to evoke the Nazi roundups which were frequent in both the occupied and non-occupied zones in France during the Second World War, suggesting that in some poems – particularly those evoking hostile intruders – Champerret must have had this contemporary context in mind, just as Ezra Pound had the vicissitudes of the First World War in mind when he translated the poems gathered in his 1915 collection *Cathay* from the Chinese.

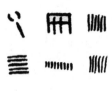

*

(a)

The sound of birds | at night | fills our ears | or is it that in
the forest | hunters imitate their calls | in the night | the hair
left | in the comb | a woman's

*

(b)

The mischievous spirit bird | of the dark pine forest | has
let down her golden hair | under cover of darkness the |
hunters gaze in wonder as she | grooms it with her comb
of moonshine | their astonished ears | in the starlight |
transfixed by her luminous song

*

(c)

The unsleeping ears | in the night | are a woman's | in the
darkness | hunters | set traps | the birds of | the forest
silenced | by rain

*

(d)

The sleeping woman | at night | hears nothing | comb hunters | come out | after dark | the hair | a forest | without birds

*

(BJ.CG.05)

*

(a)

As we sew | we hear in the distance | the stag's lonely bellow | a lone star | in the sky watches us | like the stag's eye | against the gnarled trunks | of the trees the stag | rattles its antlers

*

(b)

Needles | like fallen stars | cover the floor of the forest | a herd | of reindeer have | come over the mountains | we hear their call | see their | forked antlers raised

*

(c)

The deafening call of a stag | then out of the corner of your eye | the wrack of an antler | then suddenly the stag charges | and another and another | trampling all underfoot | the sharp needle of pain | as you fall like a star | to the forest floor

*

(d)

The antlers in | the roof of the hut | are calling | in your dream | the valley is filled | with reindeer | over the forest | snow falls | on pine needles

*

(e)

We sing the song | of the stag | as we stitch | the eye of | the stag | like a star stitch | the antlers | of the stag like | the forest of our hands

*

(f)

Above the dark forest | a star pierces the night sky | with its needles of fire | in the forest clearing | magnificent stags | numberless to the eye | the secret dance of antlers | of luminous eyes | of deep bellowing calls

*

(g)

At the forest's edge | the raised antlers | of a stag at bay | the
bright glint | in the stag's eye | like the day star | the piercing
call | of the stag | like a sharp needle

*

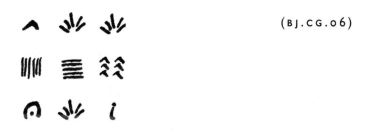

(BJ.CG.06)

*

(a)

The bright star | of the mother goddess | stares down from a
still sky | in the dark mountains | the blood stained spears of
| the hunters strike home | a canopy of stars | lights up the
settlement | the cold abandoned huts

*

(b)

The mother of the tribe has | journeyed into the mountains
| in search of a star | the star of the mother goddess | that
outshines all the | other stars | we watch the sky waiting for |
the moment she finds it | our spears idle in the huts

*

(c)

We stare out into the dark | of the night clutching our spears
| beside the empty huts | snow is tumbling | from the dark
sky | not a single star is visible | beneath a thick blanket of
snow | the silent earth mother | is sleeping in the mountains

*

(d)

We squat outside the huts | clutching our curved spears |
keeping watch | a bright shooting star | swift as an eagle |
traverses the night sky | it soars | over the black mountains |
home of the earth goddess

*

(d')

Star | over mountains

*

(e)

Above the quiet huts | a bright star flickers | like a knot in
the night sky | it is a night of many tears | a solemn mist |
covers the mountains | above the quiet huts | the lonely stars
| are weeping

*

(f)

The bright star hanging | over the black mountains | watches
us like a sleepless mother | while her unruly children | play
in the night sky | dancing and winking and shouting | as rain
begins to fall on our huts | of animal hide they drop their
toys | and turn in for the night

*

(g)

The ripe fruit | has rolled into the | glowing embers of the
fire | soon to be | extinguished | by a night of rain | at dawn
a young mother | picks up the wet fruit | sniffs it and bites

*

(BJ.CG.07)

*

(a)

From among the trees | as rain falls | the song of the birds | behind the wet huts | at the end of the track | the face of a woman | heading for the black mountains | she journeys | into the darkness

*

(b)

Hidden among trees | a single hut | in the blue mountains | it has been raining | on the winding track | all the way up | the sorrowful song | of a woman | in the night air

*

(c)

A love song | fills the | night air | rain falls | on the track | to the forest | sheltered by trees | the huts are as | quiet as the mountains

*

(c')

Song | night | rain

*

(d)

In the silence of the night | we quietly sing | our love songs |
as we climb | the winding and | rain soaked track | through
the black mountains | our huts far behind us | the tree spirits
watching

*

(d')

At night | we sing | love songs | as we walk | through
mountains | amongst tree spirits

*

(e)

The sad song | of the rain | in the pine trees | half sleeping a
woman | watches the hunters | sharpen their spears outside
the huts | they are preparing | for their night journey | into
the blue mountains

*

(f)

We build | new huts | among the trees | our trek | along
the track | in the rain is over | as night falls | we listen to a
woman | singing

*

(f')

Huts | night | woman | singing

*

(g)

The mountains | move | in the night | our huts shake | as do
the hunters | the women | the trees bend | under heavy rain |
no birds sing

*

(g')

Mountains | move | huts shake

*

*

(b)

The hunters are fired up | waving their spears | by the river | among the trees | the silhouettes | of the others | can be seen | emerging from the mist | with steady steps

*

(b')

Hunters | spears | others

*

(c)

In the sky | the mist | dances | above the trees | it forms silhouettes | of people | fire | spears | rivers

*

(e)

A mossy hut | bordered by lichen covered oaks | more moss covered huts beyond | just visible through the dawn mist | the dark pine forest | in silhouette | the flat webbed footprints | of the river people | who have departed

*

(f)

Suddenly into the still | river bed | thudding spears of fire | the dark silhouettes of the hunters | stand tall before the

swaying | branches of the trees | their heavy footsteps |
throw swirling clouds of sand | into the eyes of the fish

*

*

(a)

Cutting through the black mountains | the dried out river
bed | has become a stony track | by the silent waterfall |
there is no life | there is no birdsong | we huddle together in
the cold | of the night waiting for the sun | waiting for the
rain the light

*

(b)

Bison gather | by the waterfall | at night | along the river |
birdsong | as the sun rises | the hunters | make their chants |
as the light rises

*

(d)

The burnt out forest is still and silent | there is no birdsong
no howling of wolves no rustle of leaves | the track is a line
of ash skirting charred stumps | as the pale sun rises behind
the ash cloud | there are no birds wading at the river crossing
| no fish leap from the river's blackness | in the deathly
silence of the night | only the mournful roar of the waterfall
| can be heard from the distant black mountains

FROM *BOÎTE ROUGE: CARNET BLEU* (C)[21]

(BR.CB.002; BR.CB.012-022)

The hunters
have left
for the land
of the horses

left their huts
to take the long track
over the mountains
to the river valley beyond

mothers
look out
anxiously
over the hills

some of them
will return as men
some will return
transformed into horses

*

The hunters | have returned | as | horses | when they cry out
| we hear | the voices | of horses | when they enter the river
| we see | their horse | forms | when they see | a big cat |
they run | like horses

---

21 A selection from Champerret's variants. See note to *Boîte Rouge: Carnet Bleu* (A)

*

manhorseeyewife
wifehorseeyehorse
eyeeyewifetears
eyeeyehorsetears

*

The man | horse | sits by the fire | holding a flute | the
people | round the fire | watch | the man horse | when the
man | horse | plays | the flute | the people | hear | the birds
| the trees

*

The man who has become a horse
sits on his bottom by the fire and begins his whinnying song

he calls out softly filling the night air with his song
of the far off land of the horse people

where the lush river valley is protected
by high mountains by dense pine woods

where each day the sun goddess
watches over the horses from the peaks

*

The man who has become a horse
sings softly of the far off land of the horse people

where the grass is thick and plentiful
on the wide plain

where the fish are fat and plentiful
in the bright river

where the birds are strong and plentiful
in the clear sky

*

manhorsesonghorse
goatgoatgrassgrass
bearbearforestnight
catcatbushbush

*

The man | horse | sings of the | land of the horses | where
the | sky | is a necklace | of fire | where the shadows | of
the bison | at dawn | are as long as the river | where the |
mammoths | are as tall | as mountains

*

The man
who is now
changed into
horse form

enters the dark
and narrow tunnel
that leads into the
heart of the cave

by the flickering
light of a lamp
he sees the great
charging bulls

the glossy bulk
of the bison
the light footed reindeer
sketched in outline

by the flickering
light of a lamp
he makes out
the brightly coloured

forms of horses
galloping across the
vertiginous walls
of the cave

he looks in
wonder and with
longing at the horses
flying overhead

he neighs then
neighs again listening
to his echo as it
fades in the darkness

*

The horse man accompanies the hunters
on an expedition into the black mountains

the hunters are following the tracks
of a herd of reindeer through the pines

when they see the reindeer at rest
amongst the trees the hunters hurl their sharp spears

later when they get back to the village they look about
but can see no trace of the horse man who has vanished like
   the light

(BR.FD.05-06)

One day the hunters set out on the long path to the black mountains. As they approached the summit they saw a creature they had never set eyes on before, a monstrous winged bison. Its call was like thunder, its eyes like burning fire. It dropped down from the sky on powerful wings and carried off a mountain goat. The hunters hurled their bone tipped spears at the creature, but it dropped down from the sky once more like a great rock from out of the heavens and carried one of them off. Its call was like thunder, its eyes like burning fire. Then the weary hunters took the long path back from the black mountains to the plain.

When they got back to the village the hunters told the people about the monstrous winged bison. Its call, they said, was like thunder, its eyes like burning fire. Then the shaman put on his feathered head dress and danced wildly round the fire. Later, in his head dress, the shaman took the sloping path to the place of sacrifice, where he slit the throats of two mountain goats with his sharp blade of flint.

The next day the hunters set out again on the long path to the black mountains. They saw no trace of the monstrous winged bison they had seen before, they saw no trace of any deer or any mountain goats. Then the weary hunters took the long path back from the black mountains to the plain. At night the monstrous winged bison came down from the black mountains. Its call was like thunder, its eyes like burning fire. The creature smashed up all the huts in the settlement with its sharp horns, then seizing a girl child in its talons flew off into the black mountains. In the dark of the night the eyes of the people filled with salt tears. The bright eyes of the mothers and the fathers filled with salt tears, the bright eyes of the boys and the girls filled with salt tears. In the dark of the night the eyes of the shaman in his feathered head dress filled with salt tears.

The shaman picked a watchman, a trusted friend, to protect the village at night. The hunters laid traps in the forest and on the plain to catch the beast. They erected a wall of sharp spears round the edge of the village, fixing them fast in the dry earth, and they lit great fires which they kept burning all through the night. At dawn, when the last of the fires was almost out, the winged beast came down from the black mountains. It smashed down the wall of spears in a moment with a swish of its tail, it smashed all the huts in the village in another moment with its sharp horns, then seizing a boy child in its talons flew off into the black mountains.

In his feathered head dress the shaman took the sloping path to the place of sacrifice, where he slit the throats of two mountain goats with his sharp blade of flint. Then he took the long path past the bright waterfall into the black mountains to search out the monstrous winged bison. The shaman did not come back from the black mountains. For a whole day, for two whole days, the shaman did not come back from the black mountains. At sunset on the second day, as they looked out across the plain, the eyes of the people filled with salt tears. The bright eyes of the mothers and the fathers filled with salt tears, the bright eyes of the boys and the girls filled with salt tears. At daybreak, armed with sharp bone tipped spears, the hunters took the long path past the bright waterfall into the black mountains to search out the monstrous winged bison.

The hunters did not come back from the black mountains. For a whole day, for two whole days, the hunters did not come back from the black mountains. At sunset on the second day, as they looked out across the plain, the eyes of the people filled with salt tears. The bright eyes of the mothers and the fathers filled with salt tears, the bright eyes of the boys and the girls filled with salt tears. At daybreak, a boy and a girl took the long path into the black mountains to search out the monstrous winged bison. In the black mountains the boy and the girl listened out for the cry of the beast. They listened in silence until at last they heard its distant roar like thunder echoing from the peaks. Then they followed their ears up the long winding track to the mouth of a dark cave. They stepped into the cave's darkness. Inside they could see nothing at first, for it was as dark as death itself, but when their eyes adjusted to the darkness of the cave they saw the monstrous form of the winged bison stretched out beneath a rocky shelf, sleeping. The boy and the girl approached in silence, then quietly took their bone tipped spears and plunged them into the fiery eyes of the beast. The dying beast let out a cry like distant thunder, then took the long winding track to the shining stars, where it rests to this day. Then the boy and the girl, holding their sharp bone tipped spears out in front of them, advanced slowly into the dark heart of the cave, and then the girl sudddenly heard the quiet voices of the hunters, and the whispering of the shaman, and the small voices of the girl child and the boy child.

The boy and the girl and the hunters and the girl child and the boy child and the shaman, wearing his feathered head dress, took the long track down from the black mountains, past the bright waterfall, to the open plain. All the villagers, the men and the women, the boys and the girls, came out of their huts to greet them, and the bright eyes of the people filled with salt tears. The bright eyes of the mothers and the fathers filled with salt tears, the bright eyes of the boys and the girls filled with salt tears.

That night the shaman picked up his flute of bone and put on his feathered head dress. Then he blew gently on his flute and danced wildly round the fire in his feathered head dress like a firebird. And as he danced, the people began to chant.

The boys and the girls chanted, the fathers and the mothers chanted, and the chidren too chanted.

eye	bull	dance
eye	bison	journey
hut	necklace	dance

*

The eyes
of the bull
are dancing

the hunter
is looking out for bison
preparing for the journey

in my [?] hut
I put [?] on my necklace
ready for the dance

---

22 For reasons of economy of space, only the first and the third of
Champerret's stanzaic variations of these loose leaf drafts have been
included here. The reader who wishes to consult the full drafts, along
with some other more fragmentary poems not included here, can find
them in the manuscripts held at the Pôle de la Préhistoire in Les Eyzies.

*

The shining eyes
    of the black bull
        are dancing in the dark

the silent eyes of the hunter
    scour the horizon for ~~signs of~~ bison
        in preparation for the hunt

inside my hut [?] of deerskin
    I put [?] on my shell necklace
        ready for the night dance

man	path	cave
flint	hut	bird
grass	eye	woman

*

The man
goes into
the cave

with flint
he carves a hut
a bird

grass
~~an eye~~ eyes
a woman

*

The man sets off on
    the straight track that leads
        to the mouth [?] of the cave

he takes hold of his flint ~~burin~~
    and begins to carve the outlines
        of a hut a bird

~~he carves~~ grass blowing in the wind
an eye looking out of the rock
the body of a woman

flint	man	mammoth
spear	spear straightener	flint
river	bush	vulva

*

With his flint
the man carves
a mammoth

a spear
a spear straightener
a flint

a river
a bush
a vulva

*

Taking hold of his flint ~~burin~~
    the man begins to carve the outline
        of a woolly mammoth

he carves a not quite straight spear
    a decorated spear straightener
        a sharp pointed flint

he carves a river valley
    a bush full of berries [?]
        the outline of a woman's vulva

birds	plain	shoot
hunters	plain	birds
needle	fire	necklace

*

The birds ~~have~~
come to the plain
to feed on the shoots

the hunters ~~have~~ set off
down the river ~~valley~~
to chase the birds

we sit with our needles
round the fire
making necklaces

*

---

23 Apart from the final stanza, and some minor textual variations, this poem is identical to one of the others included in Champerret's manuscript in all its details (See *Boîte Noire: Carnet Noir* 80 below). The ending here is more arbitrary, but typical of Champerret's reading of Ice Age poetry in its understated emphasis on the everyday activities of Paleolithic peoples.

Flocks of white birds have descended
    on the river valley
        to feed on the new green shoots

the hunters have set off in pursuit
    running down the valley with their spears
        to chase the birds

we sit with our sharp needles of bone
    round the warm glow of the fire
        making necklaces from ~~pierced~~ seashells

eye	girl	star
hunters	spears	night
bear	dance	forest

*

The eye
of the girl
is like a star

---

24 Alongside a number of other poems included here (numbers 07-14), this one appears to be composed by collaging together stanzas from other poems in the Champerret manuscript. Here, arguably, Champerret strays into rare anachronism, by employing the principles of a modernist collage technique that seems unlikely to have been at the disposal of Paleolithic poets. This said, the consonance between Paleolithic parietal art and the art of modernism is beyond doubt – the direct influence on Picasso among a host of other artists, indeed, is well attested, so perhaps it is not beyond all reasonable doubt that Ice Age poetry could have anticipated techniques which were only to come to full fruition with modernism, and, indeed, postmodernism. Unquestionably, the technique here exploited by Champerret, anticipates the cut-up technique employed by Burroughs and Gysin by several decades.

hunters
throw spears
into the night

the bears
are dancing
in the forest

*

The bright blue eyes
    of the young girl
        are like stars shining in the night

the expectant hunters
    launch their flint tipped spears
        into the night air

the cave bears
    begin their dance
        in the depths of the forest

woman	river	pot
woman	sky	night
woman	cave	waterfall

*

She is
in the river
and in the pot

she falls
from the sky
when it is night

she is in the
cave but also
at the waterfall

---

*

She is found loitering
    at the river crossing
        and is never far from the cooking pot

she sometimes appears
    out of the sky
        under cover of darkness

she is found hidden in the depths
    of the cave where she sings sweetly
        but is also to be seen at the waterfall

grass   shade   woods
star   birds   river
antlers water   trees

*

Grass rustles [?]
in the shade
of the woods

stars
like birds
fly over the river

~~their~~ antlers
above the water
like trees

*

The spring grasses rustle
   beneath the shade
      of the dark oak [?] ~~woods~~

---

26 For BN.FD.07-14, see note to BN.FD.05 above.

bright flying stars
    like migrating white birds
        pass high over the river

~~their~~ horned black antlers
    rise out of the water
        like a ~~whole~~ forest on the move

mammoth	mammoth	mammoth
spears	night	mountains
man	journey	mines

*

The mammoths
have
arrived

like spears
in the night
from over the mountains

the men
have gone on a journey
to the mines

*

A herd of woolly mammoth
    have arrived crashing
        into the valley

like so many bright spears
    ~~penetrating the darkness~~
        from over the black mountains

the men of the village have departed
making the long journey over the hills
to the place where the flint lives

woman	needle	hand
people	hut	hut
night	hunters	forest

*

A woman
holds a needle
in her hand

people
gather
outside the huts

it is night
the hunters are
in the forest

*

A woman is holding
   a bone needle carefully
      between her finger and thumb

the people of the tribe
   muster ~~hurriedly~~ muster [?]
      outside the hide covered huts

night has long fallen
    and the morning hunting party
        have not returned from the forest

shaman	fire	flute
boy	path	river
man	path	cave

*

The shaman is
sitting by the fire
playing his flute

boys
take the path
to the river

a man
goes into
the cave

*

With only a single feather in his hair
   the shaman is sitting quietly by the fire
      playing his carved flute of bone

the boys follow the path to the river crossing
    to begin the ritual washing
        that precedes the sacrifice

alone a man sets off on
    the straight track that leads
        to the mouth of the cave

needle	fire	necklace
snow	snow	snow
mammoth	crossing	night

*

We sit with our needles
round the fire
making necklaces

snow
has fallen
everywhere

a single mammoth
by the crossing
as night falls

*

We sit with our sharp needles of bone
 round the warm glow of the fire
  making necklaces from ~~pierced~~ seashells

a white blanket of snow
 has fallen in the night
  covering the river valley

an isolated mammoth
    grazes by the river crossing
        as night begins to fall

shaman	night	hut
hunters	journey	village
spear	spear	spear

*

The shaman
at night
enters his hut

the hunters
have returned
to the village

they
are holding
spears

*

When night is approaching
    the shaman puts aside his magic
        enters his hut and rests

empty handed the overnight
  hunting party has returned
   to the quiet village

in their right hands
  they are holding
   sturdy bone tipped spears

hunters	trap	crossing
woman	eyes	branch
girl	comb	hair

*

The hunters
lay a trap
by the crossing

women
are looking for
branches

a girl
combs
her hair

*

The hunters have laboured since dawn
   setting up fish traps with stones and
      wooden stakes by the river crossing .

the women have gone out
     to lend a hand looking for
          sturdy branches leafy branches

tilting her head to one side
     watching a young girl combs
          her long black hair

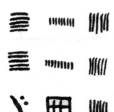

mist	silhouettes	spears
night	hunters	forest
woman	comb	hair

*

Out of the mist
they appear
carrying spears

it is night
the hunters are
in the forest

a [?] woman [?]
combs [?]
her [?] hair [?]

*

Suddenly we see their forms
   appear out of the grey mist
      carrying long bone tipped spears

night has long fallen
   and the morning hunting party
      have not returned from the forest

a [?] woman [?] sits [?] alone
   methodically [?] combing [?] her [?]
       long [?] fine [?] hair [?]

bison	flight	trees
hunters	eye	eye
~~bison~~	black	river

*

Bison
are flying
through the trees

the
hunters
watch

they are
like a
black river

*

---

27 Another poem which, apart from the final stanza, is identical to one
of the others included in Champerret's manuscript in all its details (See
Boîte Noire: Carnet Noir 88).

Horned black bison
    are flying through
        the black forest

the hunters watch
    their spears useless
        before such might

they are like
    a raging river
        in the night

night   sky   star
eye   deer   sky
trap   enemies club

*

At night
the sky is
filled with stars

I see
a deer
in the sky

a trap
enemies
a club

*

At night the sky
        is illuminated with
                a thousand bright stars

gazing up into the
        vastness I see the
                outline of a deer

I see a giant trap
    painted with stars
        enemies a great club

night	sky	star
eye	plain	sky
trees	hut	vulva

*

At night
the sky is
filled with stars

I see
a river valley
in the sky

trees
a hut
a vulva

*

At night the sky
    is illuminated with
        a thousand bright stars

gazing up into the
    vastness I see the
        outline of a river valley

I see a pine forest
    painted with stars
        a hut a giant vulva

night   rain   rain
rain   rain   rain
mountains trees huts

*

It is night
it is
raining

it is
raining
raining

on the mountains
the trees
the huts

*

It is past midnight
    it is still raining
        on the .... land

it is raining
     ~~without let up~~ in the darkness
          the cold the night

it is raining on the black mountains
     ~~it is~~ raining on the ~~tall~~ pines
          ~~it is~~ raining on the silent huts

mammoth	mammoth	waterfall
bush	eyes	spears
birdsong	birdsong	trees

*

The mammoths
are grazing
by the waterfall

from the bushes
we watch them
clutching our spears

the only sound
is the birdsong
~~coming~~ from the trees

*

The woolly mammoths
   are grazing peaceably
      beneath the bright waterfall

crouched behind bush cover
    we watch their every movement
        clutching ~~our~~ spears tight

the only sound
    is that of the birdsong
        in the forest [?]

FROM *BOÎTE JAUNE: FEUILLES DÉTACHÉES* (10-12)

The

bright blue

eyes

of the

young

GIRL

are like

sunlight in

WATER

the dark

EYE

of the
woman
in mourning

RED

is like

the endless

falling rain

the vigilant   EYES

as they

                              track

                                        are like

of the hunters

their prey

FLINT HEADED   *spears*

(BR.FD.07-09)

The bears came down in their hundreds from the distant black mountains. The hunters saw them first, coming through the dark pines. All the birds along the river bank took flight into the turbulent air, so that the whole sky, from the mountains to the hills, turned black as the night. When you looked towards the narrow river crossing, there were black bears everywhere. When you looked out across the flat plain, there were black bears everywhere. Looking up towards the bright waterfall, the place was crowded with black bears, and when you peered into the shade of the woods, there was nothing but black bears there too.

The shaman put on his feathered head dress and went down the narrow track to meet the black bears. When he encountered the bears his spirit took flight for the stars. The dark eyes of the mother of the shaman filled slowly with tears and the dark eyes of the father of the shaman filled slowly with tears. The shaman's woman in her feathered head dress went down the narrow track to meet the black bears. When she encountered the bears her spirit took flight for the stars. The dark eyes of the mother of the shaman's woman filled slowly with tears. The dark eyes of the father of the shaman's woman filled slowly with tears. The young girls put on their necklaces of bone and went down the narrow track to meet the black bears. When they encountered the bears their spirits took flight for the stars. The dark eyes of the mothers of the girls filled slowly with tears and the dark eyes of the fathers of the girls filled slowly with tears. The hunters took their flint tipped spears and went down the narrow track to meet the black bears. When they encountered the bears their spirits took flight for the stars. The dark eyes of the mothers of the hunters filled slowly with tears. The dark eyes of the fathers of the hunters filled slowly with tears. Then the dark eyes of all the people of the village filled slowly with tears. The dark eyes of the mothers of the village filled slowly with tears, the dark eyes of the fathers of the village filled slowly with tears, and the dark eyes of the boys of the village, and of the few remaining girls of the village, filled slowly with tears.

The people of the village, young and old, took shelter in their huts of deerskin. The men and the women, the boys, and the few remaining girls, took shelter in their huts of deerskin. But the black bears came up the narrow track and trampled the huts of deerskin down. The people of the village, young and old, took shelter behind the bushes of the plain. The men and the women, the boys, and the few remaining girls, took shelter behind the bushes of the plain. But the black bears came down the narrow track and trampled the bushes of the plain down. The people of the village, young and old, took shelter beneath the overhanging rocks. The men and the women, the boys, and the few remaining girls, took shelter beneath the overhanging rocks. But the black bears came up the steep slope and drove them away. Then the dark eyes of the people of the village filled slowly with tears. The dark eyes of the mothers of the village filled slowly with tears, the dark eyes of the fathers of the village filled slowly with tears, and the dark eyes of the boys of the village, and of the few remaining girls of the village, filled slowly with tears.

Now the light of the sun was beginning to fade, and the black bears took the narrow track leading into the darkness of the cave. In the night the people of the village, young and old, took the sloping path to the narrow river crossing. The men and the women, the boys, and the few remaining girls, took the sloping path to the narrow river crossing. In the night the people of the village, young and old, took the winding path to the bright waterfall. The men and the women, the boys, and the few remaining girls, took the winding path to the bright waterfall. In the night the people of the village, young and old, took the long path into the black mountains. The men and the women, the boys, and the few remaining girls, took the long path into the black mountains.

In the high mountains, from the trees of the forest, the people made wooden huts, covering them with leaves and moss. They looked out from the wooden huts covered with leaves and moss, but saw no black bears. They listened out from the wooden huts covered with leaves and moss, but heard no black bears. When they listened out from the wooden huts covered with leaves and moss they heard only the birds, singing sweetly in the pines.

The next day the pine forest was covered in crisp snow. The people of the village, young and old, lit fires with flints to keep themselves warm. The men and the women, the boys, and the few remaining girls, lit fires with flints to keep themselves warm. They scattered far and wide looking for tender roots to put in the cooking pot. The men and the women, the boys, and the few remaining girls, scattered far and wide looking for tender roots to put in the cooking pot. They scattered far and wide looking for ripe berries to put in the cooking pot. The men and the women, the boys, and the few remaining girls, scattered far and wide looking for ripe berries to put in the cooking pot. All through the winter they stayed in the pine forest. They scattered ever farther and ever wider looking for tender roots to put in the cooking pot. The men and the women, the boys, and the few remaining girls, scattered ever farther and ever wider looking for tender roots to put in the cooking pot. All through the winter they stayed in the black mountains. They scattered ever farther and ever wider looking for ripe berries to put in the cooking pot. The men and the women, the boys, and the few remaining girls, scattered ever farther and ever wider looking for ripe berries to put in the cooking pot.

When at last the long cold night of winter came to an end, and the sun shone once more in the sky over the pine trees and the black mountains, the people, young and old, took the long track through the pines to the wide plain. The men and the women, the boys, and the few remaining girls, took the long track through the pines to the wide plain. They followed the winding path to the bright waterfall. The men and the women, the boys, and the few remaining girls, followed the winding path to the bright waterfall. They retraced the path to the narrow river crossing. The men and the women, the boys, and the few remaining girls, retraced the path to the narrow river crossing. When the people, young and old, saw the ruins of the village they wept. The dark eyes of the mothers of the village filled slowly with tears. The dark eyes of the fathers of the village filled slowly with tears. The dark eyes of the boys of the village, and of the few remaining girls of the village, filled slowly with tears.

The people, young and old, took the narrow path leading to the darkness of the cave. The men and the women, the boys, and the few remaining girls, took the narrow path leading to the darkness of the cave. The black bears, they saw at once, had long departed, taking the long path to the stars, leaving only a pile of stripped bones, and the marks of their paws on the rocks.

FROM *BOÎTE ROUGE: CARNET BLEU* (F)[28]

                                    (BR.CB.037)

bear

*

A bear

*

The mark of a bear

*

The marks of a bear cub on bark

*

                                    (BR.CB.038)

mammoth

*

A mammoth

*

---

28 See note to *Boîte Rouge: Carnet Bleu* (E) above.

A mammoth by the mouth of the cave

*

The sound of a mammoth by the mouth of the cave

*

~ ◡

ﾷ ﾊ

(BR.CB.068)

birdpot
birdstrees

*

A bird in the pot birds in the forest

*

A bird in the cooking pot six birds in the trees

*

A bird cooking in the pot is worth six in the trees

*

𒌋 𒈠

𒑐 𒐼

birdsrivercrossing
huntersspears

*

Birds at the river crossing the hunters with their spears

*

When the birds gather at the river crossing the hunters pick
up their spears

*

When the birds flock together at the narrow river crossing it
is time for the hunters to pick up their spears

*

thunder

*

The thunder

*

The thunder in the distant mountains

*

The rumble of thunder in the distant mountains as night falls

*

╳   (BR.CB.119)

spider

*

The spider

*

The spider in the mouth of the cave

*

The spider in the mouth of the cave patiently rebuilding its
    web

*

ˌ˙ˌ˒   (BR.CB.120)
ˌ

footprint

*

The footprints

*

The footprints of birds in the mud

*

The footprints of birds in the mud like hand prints on the
     cave wall

*

                                   (BR.CB.123)

feather

*

The feather

*

The feather on the track to the mountains

*

The feather on the track to the mountains left by the
     departed birds

*

𝔐   (BR.CB.124)

trap

*

The trap

*

The trap concealed in the woods

*

The trap concealed in the woods waiting for the deer to come

*

(BR.CB.125)

mammoth

*

The mammoth

*

The mammoths grazing on the plain

*

The mammoths grazing on the plain still as megaliths

*

J

paw print

*

The paw print

*

The paw print of a bear on the track

*

The paw print of a bear on the track the silence of the
mountains

*

ⅢⅢⅢ

silhouettes

*

Silhouettes

*

Silhouettes in the mist

*

Silhouettes in the mist trees swaying in the breeze

*

(BR.CB.128)

birdsong

*

Birdsong

*

Birdsong at the waterfall

*

Birdsong at the waterfall first sign of spring

*

(BR.CB.129)

necklace

*

A necklace

*

A necklace of seashells

*

A necklace of seashells gift of the ocean

*

"₁ {₁₁   (BR.CB.130)

thunder

*

Thunder

*

Thunder in the hills

*

Thunder in the hills the voice of the storm

*

ᖰ   (BR.CB.131)

lamp

*

Lamp

*

Lamp light

*

Lamp light bringing the pictures to life

*

(BR.CB.132)

fish

*

Fish

*

Fish leaping at the waterfall

*

Fish leaping at the waterfall on their way to the mountains

FROM *BOÎTE JAUNE: FEUILLES DÉTACHÉES* (19–21)

is like a   STAR

The

dark

EYE

of a
turning
woman

enfolded by the night

the

cas

cad

ing

ha

ir

of

a

wo

man

at sunset   is like

the glimmer　　　of a waterfall　　　in the forest glade

the sharp

bared

of a woman

in

TOOTH

ANGER

is like a   hidden knife   of bone

FROM *BOÎTE NOIRE: CARNET NOIR* (67-99)

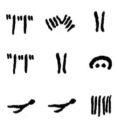

hunters	trap	river crossing
hunters	river crossing	eyes
fish	fish	spears

*

The hunters
set up a trap
by the river crossing

they stand
and watch
the water

when the fish come
they are met by
spears

*

The hunters have
set up a fish trap
by the river crossing

they stand and wait
watching for movement
in the water

when the fish arrive
they are met by
a rain of spears

*

The hunters have worked since dawn
    fixing stones and
        stakes by the crossing

when they have finished
    they stand and wait
        watching for the slightest movement

when the fish arrive first in ones and twos
    then all at once they are met by
        the thud of harpoons

rain	rain	huts
woman	eyes	branch
wood	hut	hut

*

The hard rain
has flattened
the huts

the women
are looking for
branches

and wood
to make
new huts

*

The heavy rains
that fell through the night
have flattened the huts

the women have gone out
looking for strong branches
leafy branches

and good wood
so that we can begin
the new huts

*

The fierce storm that came
    in the night
        has flattened the huts

the women have gone out
    into the forest
        looking for strong branches

and good straight wood
    to bring back
        for the new huts

night	star	sky
dawn	mist	sky
eye	mist	star

*

At night
a single star
is visible in the sky

at dawn
mist fills
the air

visible through
the mist
the same star

*

In the night
a single bright star
is visible in the sky

when dawn comes
the air is filled
with a dense mist

visible through the mist
as it begins to rise
the same star

*

In the darkness of the night
    a single bright star
        is visible in the still sky

when dawn comes with cold hands
    the air is filled
        with a dense <u>white mist</u>

just visible through the mist
    as it begins to rise [?]
        the same bright star

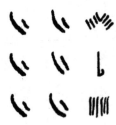

antlers	deer	head dress
antlers	reindeer	spear thrower
antlers	stag	spears

*

From the antlers
of the deer
we make a head dress

from the antlers
of the reindeer
we make a spear thrower

from the antlers
of the stag
we make spears

*

From the curved antlers
of the deer
we make a decorative head dress

from the sturdy antlers
of the reindeer
we make a decorated spear thrower

from the straight antlers
of the stag
we make pointed spears

*

From the fine curved antlers
    of the red deer
        we make a ceremonial [?] head dress for the dance

from the sturdy spiked antlers
    of the fallen reindeer we make
        a spear thrower carved with the eye of a hawk

from the long straight antlers
    of the mighty stag
        we make sharp spears for the hunt

night	eyes	bush
night	eyes	trees
night	eyes	hills

*

At night
there are eyes
in the bushes

at night
there are eyes
in the trees

at night
there are eyes
in the hills

*

At night
there are bright eyes
in the bushes

at night
there are blinking eyes
in the trees

at night
there are dark eyes
in the hills

*

In the black of the night
    there are bright eyes
        moving in the bushes

in the black of the night
    there are blinking [eyes]
        looking down from the trees

in the black of the night
    there are dark eyes
        looking out from the hills

mourner	tears	burial site
mourner	tears	cave
hut	paw print	eyes

*

There are mourners
crying
at the burial site

there are mourners
crying
at the cave

outside the hut
the paw print
is still visible

*

There are mourners
crying bitter tears
around the site of the burial

there are mourners
crying bitter tears
outside the mouth of the cave

outside the empty hut
the paw print
is still etched in the earth

*

There are long faced mourners
    crying sad and bitter tears
        around the site of the burial

there are long faced mourners
    crying sad and bitter tears
        outside the mouth of the cave

outside the empty and silent hut
    the bear's paw print
        is still etched in the dark earth

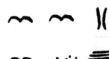

bird	bird	river
bird	footprints	water
bird	sky	call

*

Birds
flock to
the river crossing

they leave
footprints
by the water

they fill
the sky
with their calling

*

The great birds
flock together
at the river crossing

they leave
footprints behind them
by the water

they raise their sharp bills
and fill the sky
with their calling

*

The great white birds
    have come in flocks [?] to the
       river crossing

they walk up and down the bank
    leaving their footprints outlined
      in the soft mud

when they have eaten
    they raise up their heads [?] and
      fill the sky with their calling

man	path	cave
man	torch	flint
torch	flint	footprint

*

The man
goes into
the cave

he carries
a torch
and a flint

holding the torch
he takes the flint
and carves a footprint

*

The man takes
the track leading
to the cave

he carries
a torch in one hand
and a flint in the other

raising the torch in the air
he holds the flint to the wall
and carves the footprints of a bird

*

The man sets off on
    the narrow track that leads
        to the mouth of the cave

he carries a flaming
    torch in one hand
        and a flint burin in the other

raising the torch up to the cave wall
    he takes hold of the flint ~~burin~~
        and begins to carve the footprints of birds

man   path   cave
flint   antlers trees
dots   feather paw print

*

The man
goes into
the cave

with flint
he carves antlers
trees

dots
a feather
a paw print

*

The man takes
the track leading
to the cave

holding a flint to
the wall he carves
antlers trees

he carves dots
a wing feather
a bear's paw print

*

The man sets off on
    the narrow track that leads
        to the mouth of the cave

he takes hold of his flint ~~burin~~
    and he begins to carve the outlines
        of antlers of trees

he carves dots in rows
    the feather of a white bird
        the paw print of a bear

𝐼𝐼𝐼𝐼	𝐼𝐼𝐼𝐼	(sun symbol)
𝐼𝐼𝐼𝐼	𝐼𝐼𝐼𝐼	(shoot symbol)
𝐼𝐼𝐼𝐼	𝐼𝐼𝐼𝐼	(waterfall symbol)

rain	rain	sun
rain	rain	shoot
rain	rain	waterfall

*

After
the rains
the sun

after
the rains
the shoots

after
the rains
the waterfall springs to life

*

After days
of rain
the sun comes out again

after days
of rain
new shoots begin to sprout

after days
of rain
the waterfall bursts into life

*

After days of rain
    the sun comes out again
        filling the valley with its warmth

after days of rain
    green shoots burst forth
        from the dark ~~redolent~~ earth

after days of rain
    the waterfall springs into life
        filling the river with its <u>shout</u>

snow	snow	snow
grass	trees	mountains
eye	snow	footprint

*

Snow
has fallen
everywhere

covering the grass
the trees
the mountains

visible
in the snow
a single footprint

*

A white blanket
of snow has
fallen everywhere

covering the grass
the trees the mountains
all is white

the only thing visible
in the snow
the footprint of a bird

*

A white blanket of snow
    has fallen in the night
        covering the [river] valley

the grass has disappeared completely
    the trees are capped with white
        the black mountains are white mountains

the only thing visible
    in the snow as far as the eye can see
        the footprints of a bird

birds	plain	shoot
hunters	plain	birds
birds	flight	shoot

*

Birds
come to the valley
to feed on the shoots

hunters run
across the plain
to chase them

when the birds
have flown
we gather the shoots

*

Birds have come
to the river valley
to feed on the new shoots

with their spears
hunters set off
to chase them

when the frightened birds
have flown away
we follow to gather the shoots

*

Flocks of white birds have descended
   on the river valley
      to feed on the new ~~green~~ shoots

the hunters set off ~~in pursuit~~
   running down the valley with their spears
      [to chase the birds]

when the frightened birds
   ~~arrival~~ have flown away into the trees [?]
      we follow to gather the fresh green shoots

woman	head dress	shaman
woman	river	sun
woman	sky	trees

*

She is in the
head dress of the
shaman

she is on the
river in the
daytime

she is in the
sky but also
in the trees

*

She lives in
the decorated head dress
of the shaman

she is often seen
on the river
on a warm day

she is in the sky
but also at home in
the branches of trees

*

She makes her home in
    the decorated head dress
        of the ~~village~~ shaman

she is sometimes seen
    playing in the river
        when the sun is up

she can fill the sky
    blocking out the light
        but also disappear behind trees

woman	flute	fire
woman	bush	waterfall
woman	necklace	pot

*

She is in the
flute we play
round the fire

she is in
the bushes
and at the waterfall

she is also found
on a necklace
and sometimes in a cooking pot

*

Her music is in
the flute we play
round the fire

she is found
in bushes
and – often – at the waterfall

she is also found
decorating a necklace
and sometimes a cooking pot

*

Her music is heard when
    we play our slender flutes
        round the fire at night

she is found in the
    company of bushes
        and diving at the waterfall

she also likes to decorate
    a necklace and sometimes [?]
        take a dip in the cooking pot

night	bear	dance
dance	fire	chant
dawn	paw print	fire

*

In the night
bears come
to dance

they dance
round the fire
chanting

in the morning
they have gone
leaving paw prints round the fire

*

In the night the bears
came down from the mountains
to dance

they danced together round
the burning embers
growling and chanting

by morning they had gone
leaving nothing but their
paw prints round the spent fire

*

In the dark of the night
  the bears came down from the black
    mountains to perform their secret dance

all night they danced round the fire
  ecstatically [?] baring their teeth
    growling – gesticulating – chanting

by morning they had gone
  leaving nothing but their scuffed
    paw prints round the spent fire

night	trees	eyes
eyes	branch	hut
spears	knife	club

*

In the night
the trees
had eyes

they were looking
out of the branches
watching the huts

clutching their spears
their knives
their clubs

*

In the night
I dreamed the trees
had eyes

they were looking out
from between the branches
watching the sleepy huts

clutching their sharp spears
their long knives
their wooden clubs

*

In the dark of the night
    I dreamed the trees of the forest
        had green shifting eyes

they were peering out
    from between the branches
        patiently watching the huts

they clutched pointed spears
    long carved knives
        heavy wooden clubs

woman   root   shoot
woman   bush   trees
mountains   sky   pot

*

She is in
the roots
and the shoots

she is in the
bushes and
the trees

the mountains and
the sky
but also in the pot

*

She is in the
dark roots
and green shoots

she hides
in the bushes and
behind trees

she is found in the
mountains and the sky
but also in the cooking pot

*

She is found in the dark
    underground roots and in
        the sprouting green shoots

she can be found hidiing
    in bushes and sometimes
        in the heart of a tree

she is found in the mountains
    and sometimes fills the great vault of the heavens
        but also fills the cooking pot

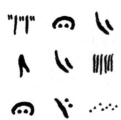

hunters	eyes	deer
wound	deer	spears
eyes	woman	dance

*

The hunters are
watching
the deer

they have
wounded it
with their spears

later they watch
the women
dancing

*

The hunters are
watching the deer
from a safe distance

with their spears
they have wounded
but not killed it

later round the fire
they will watch
the women dancing

*

The hunters are watching the deer
    from the safety of the bushes
        as it stumbles round and round

they have wounded it
    in the flank [?] from which their
        barbed spears hang like branches

later by the warmth of the fire
    they will watch the young women of the village
        as they dance round and round

〝|〝|〝 ︿ ⫼⫼

〝|〝|〝 ︿ ⫼⫼

〝|〝|〝 ︿ ⫼⫼

hunters   hut   spears
hunters   fire   spears
hunters   hut   spears

*

The hunters leave
the huts
holding their spears

they sit round
the fire
spears at their sides

they enter
the huts
holding their spears

*

The hunters leave
the huts at dawn
holding their spears

later they sit round
the bright fire
spears at their sides

at night they enter
the hut's darkness
holding their spears

*

At dawn the hunters leave their
    huts heading off into the hills
        to hunt with their long spears

later when they have returned
    from the hunt they sit round the fire
        their spears laid at their sides

at night when the day is done
    they step into the darkness of the hut
        obsessively clutching their long sharp spears

bison	flight	trees
hunters	eye	eye
bison	flight	trees

*

Bison
are flying
through the trees

the
hunters
watch

bison
are flying
through the trees

*

Black bison
are flying
through the trees

the hunters
watch clutching their
useless spears

black bison
are flying
through the trees

*

Horned black bison
    are flying through
        the black forest

the hunters watch
    their spears
        useless

horned black bison
    are [flying through]
        the black forest

woman	black	night
woman	mountains	mountains
woman	eye	needle

*

She is
black
as the night

she is
as large
as the mountains

she fits
through the eye
of a needle

*

She is black
as the darkest
night

she is as
large as a
mountain range

yet she fits
through the eye
of a needle

*

She is as black
    as the darkness
        of the night

she is as
    large as the
        tall [?] black mountains

yet she fits
    through the slender eye
        of a needle of bone

night	rain	bison
forest	river	fire
eyes	eyes	hut

*

In the night
there was a rain
of bison

the forest
and the river
were on fire

eyes were
watching me
inside the hut

*

In the night
bison fell from the sky
like rain

the pine forest
and the river
were all blazing

eyes were watching
me from the hide
walls of the hut

*

In the dark of the night
    bison fell from the sky
        like deadly rain

the trees of the pine forest
    and the waters of the river
        were all ablaze with fire

the angry eyes of dead reindeer
    were watching me from
        the pelts [?] of the tent

night   mountains   trees
eye   mammoth   fire
mammoth   torch   tusks

*

In the night
I was in the mountains
climbing trees

I saw
mammoths gathered
round a fire

they carried
torches and
brandished their tusks

*

In the night
I was in the mountains
climbing the great trees

I saw a herd
of mammoth gathered
together round a fire

they carried
torches in their mouths
and brandished their tusks

*

In the dark of the night
    I was in the black mountains
        climbing the great pines

I saw a herd of mammoth
    in conference [?] gathered
        round a great fire

they carried flaming torches
    in their mouths and brandished
        their ivory tusks like spears

night	cave	torch
eye	vulva	vulva
eye	shaman	club

*

In the night
I was in the cave
carrying a torch

I saw
a wall
of vulvas

I saw the shaman
who carried
a club

*

In the night
I dreamed I was in the cave
holding a flaming torch

I saw a wall of
vulvas carved into
the soft clay of the cave wall

I saw the eyes of the
shaman who carried
a heavy club in his hand

*

In the dark of the night
    I dreamed I entered the cave
        making my way into its heart [with a torch]

In the cave's darkness I saw
    a wall of vulvas
        carved into the surface of the rock

I saw the shaman wearing a wrack
    of antlers on his head
        in his hand he carried a club

night	sky	star
eye	paw print	sky
mammoth	fish	spear thrower

*

At night
the sky is
filled with stars

I see
a paw print
in the sky

a mammoth
a fish
a spear thrower

*

At night the sky
is filled with
a thousand stars

gazing up into the
sky I see
a paw print

I see a mammoth
a glinting fish
a spear thrower

*

At night the sky
    is illuminated with
        a thousand bright stars

gazing up into the
    vastness I see the
        paw print of a bear

I see a mammoth
    painted with stars a
        silver [?] fish a spear thrower

night   sky   star
eye   aurochs   sky
bird   needle   mother

*

At night
the sky is
filled with stars

I see
an aurochs
in the sky

a bird
a needle
a mother

*

At night the sky
is filled with
a thousand stars

gazing up into the
sky I see
an aurochs

I see a bird
a sharp needle
a mother

*

At night the sky
    is illuminated with
        a thousand bright stars

gazing up into the
    vastness I see the
        outline of an aurochs

I see a white bird
    painted [?] with stars a
        needle the great mother [?]

man	man	sun
man	woman	night
cave	man	deer

*

He is a man
when the sun
is up

he is
a woman
by night

in the cave
he is half man
half deer

*

He is a man
by day when
the sun is up

by night
round the fire
he is a woman

in the darkness of the cave
he is half man
half deer

*

He is a man
    in the light of day
        when the sun is up

by night when we sit
    [round] the fire
        he is a woman

in the dark heart
    of the cave he is
        half man half deer

night	path	river crossing
eye	eyes	fish
feather	sky	snow

*

In the night
I took the path
to the river crossing

I could see
the eyes of the
fish looking at me

feathers fell
from the sky
like snow

*

In the night
I dreamed I took the straight
track to the river crossing

I could see
the bright eyes of the
fish looking at me from the water

great white feathers fell
from the clear sky
like snow

*

In the dark of the night
    I dreamed I took the straight
        track leading to the river crossing

I could see the bright eyes
    of the fish staring at me from
        beneath the surface of the water

great white feathers from passing
    birds fell from the clear sky
        like snowfall in winter

night	fire	sky
hut	fire	wood
shaman	fire	torch

*

In the night
fire fell
from the sky

our huts
took fire
like wood

the shaman
was set alight
like a torch

*

In the night
I dreamed flaming fire
fell from the sky

our huts burst into
flames like
dry moss

the shaman's head dress
burst into flames
like a burning torch

*

In the dark of the night
    I dreamed flaming fire fell
        from the dark vault [?] of the sky

our huts of deerskin
    burst into flames
        like dry moss from the forest

the shaman ~~bedecked~~ in his
    bright head dress of feathers
        was set alight like a lliving torch

reindeer   reindeer   reindeer
reindeer   reindeer   reindeer
reindeer   reindeer   reindeer

*

Reindeer
reindeer
reindeer

reindeer
how I love you
reindeer

reindeer
reindeer
reindeer

*

Reindeer
how I
love you

reindeer
reindeer
reindeer

how I
love you .
reindeer

*

How I
   love you
      reindeer

red
   and white
      and again red

reindeer
   how I fucking [?]
      love you

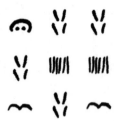

eyes	bison	bison
bison	rain	rain
bird	bison	bird

*

We are looking
out for
bison

looking for bison
in the
rain

amidst
the
birds

*

We watch out for
the red bison
on which we depend

watch out for their
glistening pelts
in the rain

among
the white
birds

*

So much depends
    upon the red bison
        from the hills

their pelts glazed
    with rain water
        in the evening sun

surrounded by
    the white birds
        of the air

From Champerret's Key to the Lascaux Signs:
Boîte Rouge: Carnet Bleu

1.   = feather, shaman

2.   = people

3.   = spear, stick, rope, flute, post, horn

4.   = eye, sky, hut

5.   = needle, lamp

6.   = people, bear

7.   = needle, woman, spirit

8.   = man, boy

9.   = woman, girl, wife, spirit

10.   = antler, deer, stag, reindeer, tusks

11.   = root

12.   = stag

13.   = divide, divide in track, fork

14.   = peg, vulva, wound

15.   = journey, footprints, dance, track, run

16.   = horns

17.   = footprint

18.   = journey, track

19.   = journey, path, track

20.   = trap, head dress

21.  = people, silhouettes, henge, hunters

22.  = bison, necklace, bull, aurochs, cow

23.  = journey, footprints, dance, dots

24.  = necklace

25.  = man, spear, torch, father, number

26.  = tooth, knife, flint

27.  = hunters

28.  = axe, club

29.  = forest track

30.  = crossing, river, river crossing

31.  = people, enemies, many

32.  = bison, mountains, crossing, huts, hills

33.  = fish

34.  = burial site, mourner, sacrifice

35.  = cave

36.  = hut, fire, burning

37.  = paw print, bear

38.  = bird, fish, antler, deer, river

39.  = forest, spears, rain, hair, sticks, tears, war

40.  = river, river valley, plain

41. = mammoth, cave, ear

42. = birdsong, horns, bird, call, song, chant, voice, bird call

43. = flint

44. = thunder

45. = mountains, mine, village

46. = trees, forest, wood

47. = mountains

48. = mist, night, shade, water, black, fog, smoke, shadow, death, darkness

49. = legs, feet, trample

50. = waterfall

51. = spear, manstick, spear thrower, spear straightener, bone straightener

52. = faces, berries, few

53. = hand, pelt

54. = branch

55. = watchman, eyes, happiness, horse

56. = tree, leaf, bush, grass

57. = wood, light, burnt forest

58. = mother, knot

59. = trap, comb, scaffold, horse

60. = beads

61. = sun, star, fruit, dawn, snow, snowflake, tear, day

62. = goat, fallen horse

63. = spider

64. = birds, spirit, soul

65. = bird, bat, flight

66. = birds, spirit, soul

67. = root

68. = cooking pot, breast

69. = bush, herb

70. = shoot

APPENDIX 2

From Champerret's Charcoal Drawings of Lascaux Signs:
Boîte Jaune: Cartes Postales

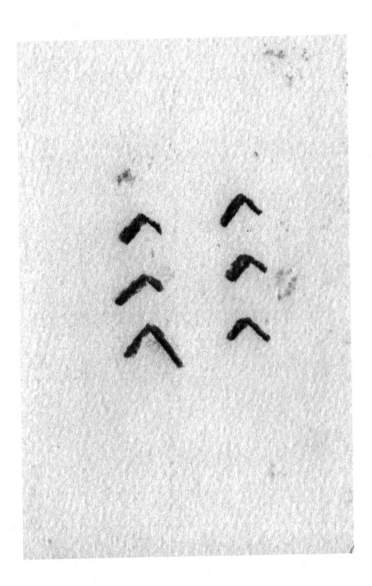

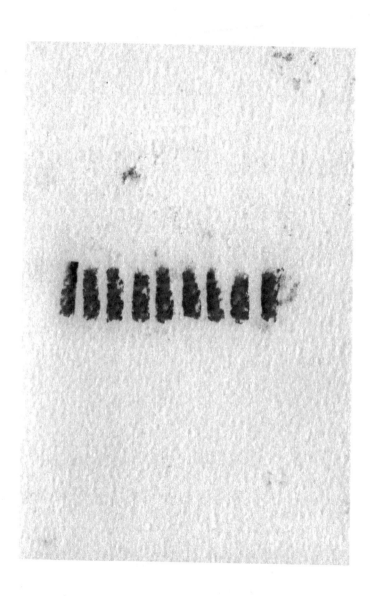

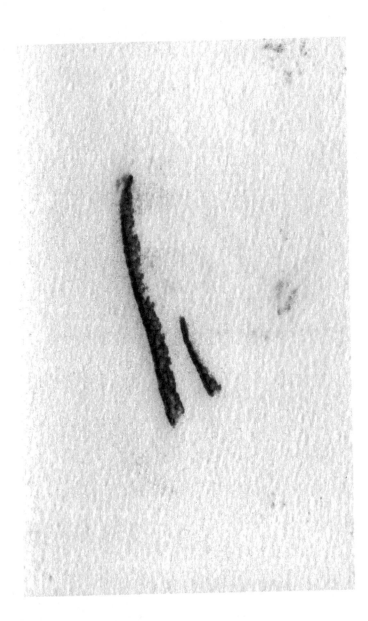

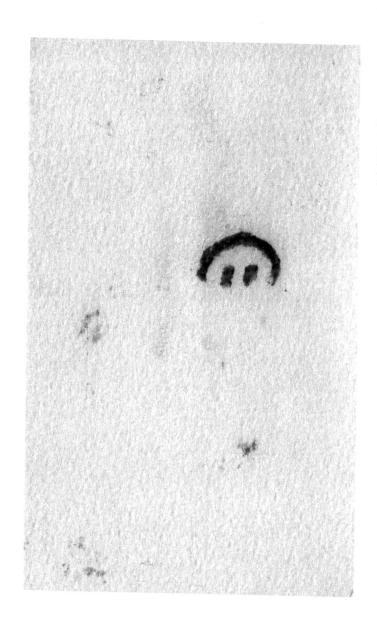

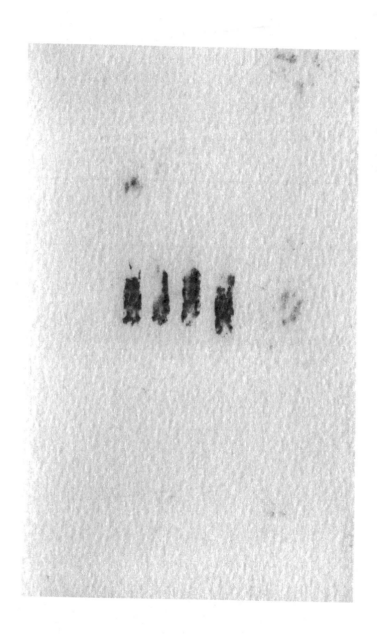

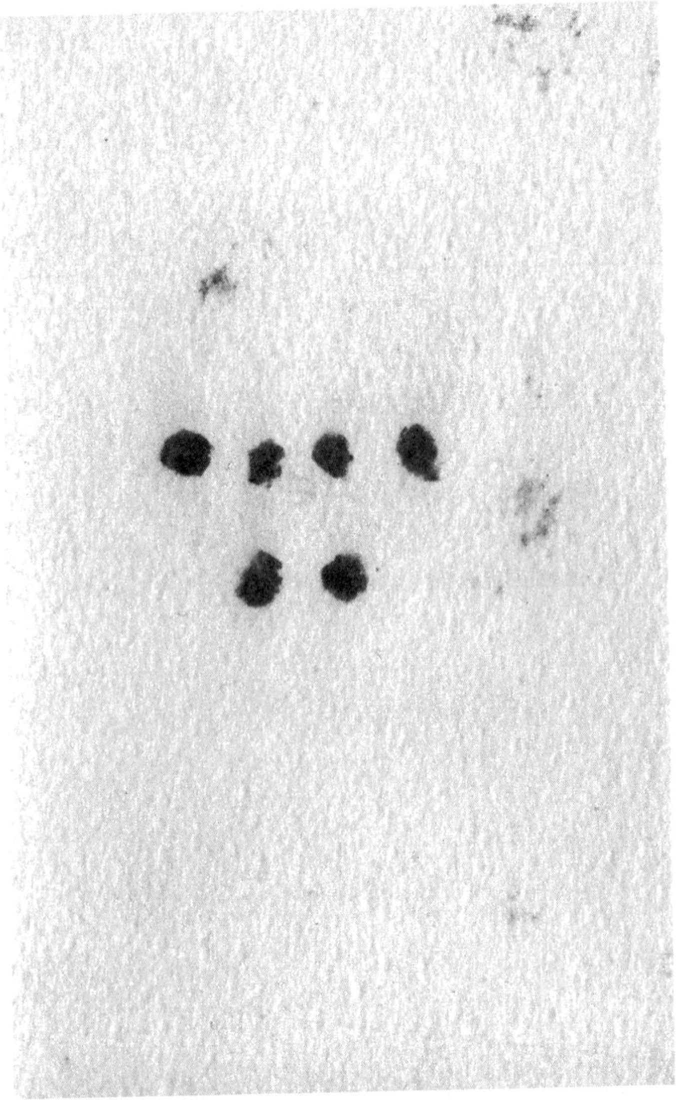

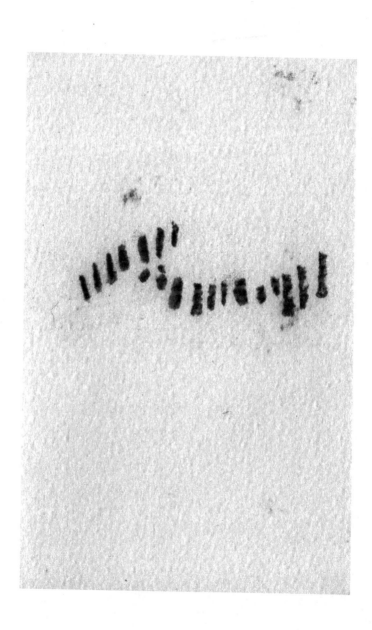

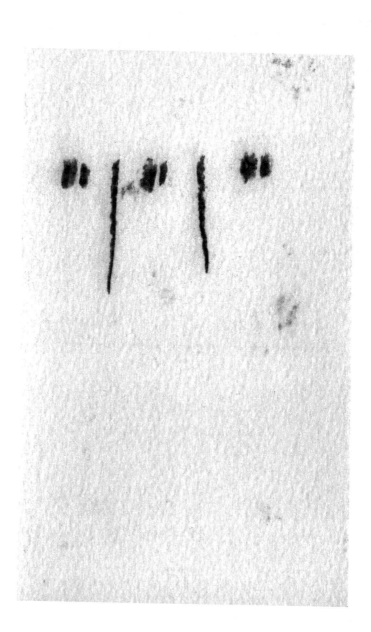

ACKNOWLEDGEMENTS

Acknowledgements are due to *PN Review* where three of Champerret's poems first appeared in this translation in May–June 2021. For conservation reasons it has not been possible to copy the drawings of Champerret directly from his notebooks, which remain fragile. For this edition Champerret's drawings of the signs and sign grids have been reproduced in ink by Lee Shearman working in collaboration with the archivists at the Pôle de la Préhistoire, Les Eyzies. The signs were originally inked using a Leonardt Copperplate nib No.5 and sepia-coloured Diamine dipping ink. Champerret's charcoal drawings of the signs have been reproduced in facsimile by Lou Terry working in collaboration with the Art Department of the Pôle de la Préhistoire, directed by Pierre Leblanc. Photography is by Paul Anderson. Thanks are due to the staff of the Pôle de la Préhistoire, in particular Annie Levallois and Pierre Leblanc, and to the Cambridge Archaeological Society and the Bean Trust who have been generous with their support. Thanks also to Jeff Hilson, Zoë Skoulding, Gregory Betts and James Davies, who invited me to present early drafts of these translations at conferences and festivals in France, Ireland and the UK. Special thanks to Iris Colomb for advice on the translation.